What's Your Purpose?

What's Your Purpose?

Seven Questions to Find Your Answer

RICHARD JACOBS

HODDER
MOBIUS

First published in Great Britain in 2004
by Hodder and Stoughton
A division of Hodder Headline

The right of Richard Jacobs to be identified as the Author
of the Work has been asserted by him in accordance with
the Copyright, Designs and Patents Act 1988.

A Mobius paperback

1 3 5 7 9 10 8 6 4 2

A CIP catalogue record for this title is available from the
British Library

ISBN 0 340 73449 3

Typeset in 10·5/15pt Stone Serif by Phoenix Typesetting,
Auldgirth, Dumfriesshire

Printed and bound in Great Britain by
Mackays of Chatham Ltd, Chatham, Kent

Hodder and Stoughton
A division of Hodder Headline
338 Euston Road
London NW1 3BH

For love to rule the world

Acknowledge-Meants

I, like the rest of us, am a collection of a lot of other people with my own bits thrown in. I have met some extraordinary teachers in my life to whom I am forever indebted. Most notably I would like to thank:

Shandor Remete, the greatest yogi I have ever encountered and a spectacular inspiration.

John De Ruiter who speaks the simplest and gentlest of truths.

Andrew Cohen who has a mind like a scalpel and in whom there burns a passionate fire of freedom.

Chuck Spezzano who loves people, intimacy and relationships and taught me the language of questions and the living metaphor.

Lita De Alberdi who showed me the landscapes and nature of light.

Kalinka Poullain, my wife and guide. She is a constant reminder to me that angels walk on earth.

I would also like to thank Julia McCutchen, Humphrey Price, Emma Heyworth-Dunn, Rowena Webb and all the team at Hodder and Stoughton.

Above and beyond my family, friends and the great people above, the people who have taught me the most have been those who have come to my seminars. I am their student. They have taught me kindness, simplicity, authenticity and the miraculous beauty of humanity. I salute and thank you.

My final thanks goes to the Shepherd who sits inside me . . .

Contents

CONTENTS

TAKING FLIGHT

We are all fundamentally the same. We all want peace, loving relationships, a sense of meaning and truth in our lives, and to feel in our autumn years that the world is somehow richer for our presence. So where does this sense of fulfilment come from? And do we have to wait until it's nearly all over before we realise what is truly important to us?

What's Your Purpose? lets you find answers to these questions by helping you to define and live what is most important to you. Purpose is a focus, an intent. *What's Your Purpose?* asks you, What do I intend to give to the world? Do you wish to leave this planet with things untried, undone and unsaid? In our heart of hearts, each of us wants to live life deeply in integrity with who we are and our highest vision of the world. Every time we go against this deep sense of knowing and 'rightness' we eat away at our own energy source and we become compromised human beings; someone who has settled for less than their best, who has become jaded, tired and believing more in limitation than in possibility.

Purpose is the acupuncture point of integrity. When we

live it, everything that is meaningful to us, our values and our highest beliefs come into alignment and we become the expression of the best part of ourselves.

A friend of mine, who eventually died of Aids, told me the following story: back in the days when it took six weeks to get the results of an Aids test, a man was convinced that he had contracted the virus. One of his previous partners was HIV positive so during the six weeks he was waiting, he made lists of all the things he wanted to do with his life: the places he would go, the people he would meet, and those with whom he would make amends. When the day of his results came he was clear about what he wanted to do. It turned out that he had not contracted HIV. He was overjoyed and had his friends round to celebrate. Over dinner he produced his lists and was just about to burn them over the candles when someone asked him what he was doing.

'I'm burning my lists. I'm going to live now. I don't need them any more.'

'But now you know what you want out of life,' his friend exclaimed.

'Yes,' he replied.

'Then why not live it? If you were going to die in a year you would have lived everything on that list. Now that you have sixty years left you may as well spend your whole life living what you want. That is the most valuable list you could have.'

I was very inspired by the story. What was ultimately important to people when they faced the end of their life?

The answers seemed clear: that they had lived according to their core values, meaning how much love they gave and received in their life. They also wanted to feel somehow that the world is richer for their presence. Don't we all want that? What would we do if only we gave ourselves the time and authority? How much of what we truly wish for ourselves do we pursue? And do we have to be on our death-beds to know what's important?

What's Your Purpose? is your map and your guide to finding out your answers to all these questions.

My Story

Purpose is my Life. For many years I thought I was an actor. Then I became a trainer. I was also a businessman, a boyfriend, a son, a brother, a friend and another guy in the street. I was all those things and more but I didn't really know who I was, and, more importantly, why was I here.

When I was four years old my burning ambition was to be Tarzan. It was all I cared about. I had some leopard-skin-patterned swimming trunks and I would dive into the pool with a plastic knife between my teeth and battle imaginary crocodiles. Tarzan was the perfect man as far as I could see. He was the balance between human and nature. He was elegant, graceful, strong, brave and noble by nature. One day, when I announced my ambitions to become king of the jungle, I was informed by a film director friend of my parents that for my dream to come true I would have to be taken away from my family and grow up in the jungle with the beasts. I would have nothing, absolutely nothing, of the life I knew. This was a serious blow to my plans. I had not considered having no bed, cooked food, baths, parents, family, holidays, cuddles and all the other important things in life.

I took two days to consider my options. Eventually I returned to my parents and friend and announced my resolution. I would do both: become my hero *and* come home at night. My plan was to become an actor. That way

I could *play* Tarzan yet still have a home life. I never changed my mind.

Sure enough I became an actor. I worked in theatre, film and television and was accounted successful but I never fully realised the wisdom I had innately as a four-year-old. In my mind as a child, I could have and be whatever I wished. There were no limits, so I simply invented the future I wanted. As I grew older though my thoughts began to be infected by the 'either/or' syndrome. *Either* I could become an actor *or* I could be successful. *Either* I could follow my heart and my passion *or* I could build a stable and secure home. *Either* I could be a trainer *or* a storyteller. In becoming a 'grown-up' I had lost my greatest gift – my ability to say 'and' not 'or'. I forgot what I knew as a child. I thought that I could not have love and lifestyle. I could not have a healthy relationship and pursue my dreams. I had compromised my greatest wishes. And of course because that was my belief, that was exactly what I got. I was a creator who had forgotten his magic. Like Dorothy in *The Wizard of Oz*, wearing her ruby slippers but not knowing how to use them, I did not know how to access my power. Without knowing it, I was living a half-life. My discovery, my journey brought me home.

It all began one day when a long-term relationship I was in ended; I was devastated. My life crumbled around me and I sank into a pit of despair the likes of which I had never known before. One night, in my anguish, beyond comfort or hope, I cried out my pain. I had never been religious, superstitious or remotely metaphysical but I just called out to anything or anyone that could diminish my pain and grief. In that moment I felt the presence of my great-aunt who had long since passed away. I could smell her and almost touch her. I felt her hands come into my body and cup my heart. She held it in her hands and stopped it breaking. I had never known love or compassion like that before and I just cried and cried . . . But I knew I was saved.

Little by little my life started to turn around, and over the next few weeks and months I started to take control – to change my life. I began to learn how to meditate. Books and leaflets found their way into my hands. I just happened to meet people who gave me the advice I needed at exactly the right time, and I was invited to participate in a training course.

It was an electrifying experience. I suddenly realised that I had so much to say. Ideas poured out of me and I discovered a healing and an understanding about life I had never been conscious of before. I devoured books on spiritual and personal growth and expanded my work and experience as a facilitator.

I worked with individuals and groups on communication, presentation skills, creativity and Attitude change. I always worked from a point of fundamental personal development and mastery because that was the only thing I was interested in. And, because I have a low boredom threshold, I devised exercises that were both enjoyable and which achieved results rapidly.

My success as a trainer grew but my ambitions as an actor were unfulfilled and never far away. I was torn between the practical and the dream. I wanted both but somehow I felt that my dreams had to take a back seat to the reality that I had to earn a living. I considered giving up my acting, thinking it was a foolish childhood fantasy, but every time I tried I felt sick and dead inside. I was constantly swinging between the two and never fully satisfied with either. Training did not give me the artistic expression I sought and the acting world was so often void of meaning that I found it hard to be genuinely and deeply motivated by a project. What was I, an actor or facilitator? Which one of these was my destiny? What did I come here to do?

It was this last question that preoccupied me. I thought about it for years until I eventually discovered that the answer was in two parts.

It's up to me to choose. I am here now, I decide what happens to my life and how. No one else can do it for me. What I am here to do is not a job, it is something much deeper than that. It is my whole reason for being and it would be the same regardless of the age I lived in or the culture. It transcends time and does not stop at death. It is my Purpose.

I have become aware that I cannot teach anybody anything and neither do I wish to. The source of knowledge for each of us lies within ourselves. I have discovered that the greatest gift I can give to others is to help them listen and follow the gentle voice of their inner being. This, I know, will always lead them where they truly wish to go. It is the source of all wisdom.

I spent two years of my life listening. Every day I would sit for two hours and simply listen . . . to myself and to the world. I placed no judgement on what I heard. As I became better at this, the simplest of skills, I started to hear my own truth. It taught me who I am and what is more important to me. I became free of my education and upbringing and started daring to live on the outside what I was thinking and feeling on the inside. It took me another year to learn how to articulate this fully in words. When I could, I knew that my words represented what was most important and meaningful to me in my life. I knew what I stood for and that I would accept nothing less. It was the Purpose of my life. As soon as I knew what it was there was no turning back. Since then my life has taken off. It was as if the discovery of my Purpose had brought me into the next stage of my journey, a stage I had been waiting to happen for years but had no idea how to trigger. I felt like I had entered into the next stage of my evolution as a human being.

Discovering my Purpose has been the most profound experience of my life, and, in some ways, the simplest. I started my love affair with life. Every part of my life improved. I became more settled, confident, creative and, most important of all, peaceful. As I was experiencing these changes I continued to work with groups and individuals, delivering presentation skills seminars. I would give participants subjects on which to talk but because of the discoveries I made through living my Purpose, I invited people to speak on what was most important to them. The changes were dramatic. People who had previously been tongue-tied and often terrified of speaking in public suddenly became charismatic, passionate and compelling presenters. Their fears simply dropped away. Was it tapping into their Purpose that was so liberating?

As I experienced more of what I felt now that I'd started living with my Purpose, I knew I wanted to help more people discover theirs. What could be more important or compelling? What would a world of Purpose-driven people be like? Since starting to put my Purpose into action, I have encountered a wealth of synchronicity and a surging tide of coincidence which have deepened my faith and commitment to the actions I'd taken to change my life to an unshakeable degree.

I realised that discovering our Purpose was a key into self-mastery but I had no idea how that could be triggered in others. I felt it was impractical to suggest to people that they spend three years of their life listening for two hours per day and contemplating their navels. It had taken me a substantial amount of effort to find my Purpose and I had to refine it to be able to pass it on. That's when I found out about geese.

My friend Dani showed me a video one day, called *Lessons from Geese*.* I had been asked to design a seminar to help a disparate group of individuals with

* Milton Olson

conflicting ambitions. There were forty-five executives in all, living and working in different geographic locations – sometimes thousands of miles apart – who were too busy building their own empires to collaborate effectively. How to get them to want to work together as one was going to be a challenge. Just as I was struggling with this, Dani showed me the video. It told me: The reason why geese fly in V formation is because as each bird flaps its wings it creates an uplift for the one that follows it. This way the whole flock achieves an extra 71 per cent flying range: 71 per cent! When the lead goose tires it drifts back into the formation and another moves to the lead position so that they all benefit from the extra lift.

It seemed to me that nature had the perfect model. These birds were working better together than any other human group I had ever met or heard of; and they have brains the size of olives. If geese can do it, I thought, I'm sure people can. I based the seminar on the geese model and found a way of helping all the participants unite behind a common Purpose. The seminar was a huge success, and I was on the way to explaining Purpose.

I learned that day, in the seminar, that *there is no relationship between effort and effectiveness*. If you or I were to swim two lengths of a swimming pool we would use much more effort than an Olympic swimmer covering the same distance. The refinement in the Olympic swimmers' style means that they can get more done with less energy. Their effectiveness is determined by their technique and the relationship between themselves and the element they are in, rather than through effort alone. Harnessing the subconscious exploits the principle that *there is no relationship between effort and effectiveness*. In our example of the swimmer, they glide effortlessly through the water because they are fully at ease with the element they are in, the aerodynamics they cause through the actions of their body. In the same way, the quality of the actions we take through our thoughts and intentions creates greater or lesser effectiveness. It's cause and effect. Our 'water' is our inner environment. Kicking with our legs is the movement of our conscious and subconscious minds. The movements of our arms are the pull of our intuition and our quality of intention. Aligning them, bringing them into the same dance brings about this effortless effectiveness.

In this book we rely heavily on the place where the subconscious mind and the intuition overlap. I call this the 'Yes Spot'. It is the acupuncture point of effortless effectiveness. People sometimes have trouble accepting this principle. We innately seem to feel that the best way to succeed at things is simply to work hard at them. However, if we had as much sense as geese, we might understand that there are ways of using our energy to give us great results and which require very little effort. In their V formation, for example, they put in 29 per cent effort, and get 100 per cent out. If they fly alone, out of integrity with their highest good, they put in 100 per cent effort to get 100 per cent out. People are the same; if you think of your 'inner geese' as the collective point around which all your values collect, when we 'fly' with our inner geese out of alignment, we are wasting the best part of ourselves, which is tiring, ineffective and unfulfilling. Whether collectively or individually, when we focus our efforts around a single Purpose, we accomplish our goals faster and with a greater sense of fulfilment and morale. If greater effectiveness and well-being comes from a single point of focus, how can that principle be applied to us all as individuals? In other words, how do we get our inner geese in order?

When I asked people the question, 'What's your Purpose?' they found it very hard to answer. However, when I asked them questions that indicated their Purpose using their creative mind, as in 'What would you do if' . . . they found it much easier.

So I put together a series of questions appealing to our imaginations to help people discover what is most important to them; their values and what they would like to have given in this lifetime. As they knew their answers to be true, their values became aligned and they started to experience the 71 per cent extra lift in their life as their inner geese flew in formation. This 71 per cent extra lift means different things to different people. What would it look like in your life? The head of the V is Purpose.

I help people listen to their truth by putting them in touch with what is meaningful to them: their Purpose. The inner voice is located in the same place as your Purpose; two rooms in the same house. When you find one, you find the other.

Over the time I have worked with my Purpose, I have learned that I am more than my job or the role I play in society. I have learned that as I live and give my values, I become Value-able to the whole. What I *do* is far less important than the focus and intention that I *give* to it; *that* becomes my experience of the world and therefore my life. I am not my job, my home, my relationship, my car. Everything I have and everything I am is an extension of me and the more I live my Purpose the more meaningful my life becomes. I have had plenty of money and I have had none, but in the end it is of little consequence. The only thing that matters is the meaning I give to my life. That is my true richness; the life-source of which is my Purpose. Were I Tarzan, life would be no greater an adventure than the one I am currently living.

Giving Purpose

The Purpose | Attitude | Means programme I designed has brought me untold benefits, so much so that I realised I wanted to share its simplicity and effectiveness with others. Over the last few years I have been testing, refining and redesigning this programme, working with large multinational organisations, members of the public, unemployed people, teachers, actors, artists, personal development seminar leaders, engineers, accountants, my wife, my brother and the person next door. The results have been astounding, deeply touching and enormously gratifying.

The programme works in three parts: arriving at your own Purpose statement; creating an Attitude that cultivates positive behaviours; using the Means section to generate your Purpose in everything you say, do and think.

People are invariably bowled over by the beauty and simple clarity of their own Purpose statements, which they often manage to articulate in five or six words. As a result of identifying their Purpose in this way, they have made significant and lasting changes in their lives, always for the better and in line with what speaks to them most.

Some have decided to marry, others have changed jobs, moved house, developed their businesses, deepened their relationships with partners, decided to have children and engaged in world-changing programmes.

The most significant effect is that they have made positive moves to bring what is most important to them to life. They start to live their lives in a way where they will have no regrets in their final hours, where, if they are asked the question at the pearly gates, 'What did you give?' they can honestly answer, 'The best of myself.'

This book is my way of giving the best of myself to the greatest number.

You and Your Purpose

When you start living your Purpose, all your values will come into line around a single focus. This is something you may never have done before in your life. Purpose is a constant direction, an inner fire of meaning that drives you. It is what is most important to you, your values, your gifts and your talents combined. That, expressed, is your Purpose. It is the grain of meaning that resides in every single thing you do. When you know what that is, its characteristics and flavour, you will not want anything else. Discovering and living your Purpose is like tasting real food for the first time after eating take-aways your whole life. It is both good for you and life tastes the way you instinctively know it should.

Everyone has values whether they know them or not. We all have talents and abilities and we all have different ways of giving the best of ourselves. Our Purpose is the combination of all three. It is impossible not to have a Purpose. All so-called 'great' people were unknown at some point in their lives; their greatness came from their commitment to their Purpose and not the other way around. Are we born great or do we become it? My view is that we become it through the quality and integrity of our actions. The people we describe as 'great' live their lives entirely devoted to their Purpose. That is what defines them and their quality of presence. The more we live our Purpose, the more it defines us and our lives.

In society we are bombarded by images, ideas and media dogma that expound how life ought to be. It should look like this, feel like this, sound like that and have all the accessories to keep it turning. None of that is true. None of it can be, since we are the only arbiters of what is right for us. How can we really know who we are unless we somehow remove ourselves from these influences and make some free choices? The key to our freedom and therefore our joy is in living our greatest truth to the full. *Our* truth has to come as a result of *our* choices. Once we find our truth and live that, everything falls into place. This is simply because we are being and expressing who we *truly* are instead of trying to buy into some 'idea' of ourselves: the real us, as opposed to the advertisement of us.

All the questions you'll encounter later in this book talk to your creative/intuitive mind. Our logical mind says how the world *ought* to be, which is heavily influenced by our upbringing, education, our peers and our own quickly drawn judgements about what is right and wrong. Your creative and intuitive mind sees how things *could* be; and that could be fantastic, practical, or both. We can watch a film or imagine a story where it is totally acceptable for animals to talk, trees to walk and the sky to have friends, yet if someone suggests the possibility of world peace within our lifetime or of having more weekend than week, more often than not people reject the possibility. Our creative imagination is free and therefore allows us the possibility of making choices unfettered by our past or the pressures of our modern society. This will be the route into our truth. Each question acts as a clue into an ever deepening, inner treasure hunt. As you respond to them in your honesty and integrity, they unravel their wisdoms and you progress on to the next until eventually you discover your diamond within: your diamond of Purpose.

Discovering and living your Purpose is the next great chapter in your life. You know who you are now, but do you know who you could be if you were to live the best of yourself and only that? I cannot tell you who you could be or what the best of you is, nobody can. Of course that won't stop parents, teachers and friends trying; everyone has an opinion, no matter how well intentioned they are. The only person who can decide who the best of you is, and what it would like to give to the world, is *you*. You have to find your own truth out for yourself. That is why this book provides questions, rather than answers. The right questions will help you find out everything you need to know and you will also see that *you* are the source of all your answers and wisdom. In this way, Purpose becomes your guiding light, your North Star. You will also discover that it is inside yourself and so you can never be lost again.

This 'coming home to yourself' is a great freedom. My yoga teacher, Shandor Remete, encourages people to work on their stance, legs and footwork. 'When your legs are strong,' he says, 'the rest can play.' When we discover and live our Purpose we get an unshakeable anchor deep inside ourselves. This helps us have the courage and capacity to play with life and to experiment with our gifts, talents and abilities. Within that play is our fullest expression. We literally go beyond ourselves and get to discover ourselves as a greater person than we ever imagined before.

The words people write as their Purpose statements hold a deep and true meaning for them, pregnant with all that they care and are most enthusiastic about. Think of it as the diamond we spoke about before. It's buried deep within us but for one reason or another we have never looked for it. This process helps us locate the diamond and your Purpose statement *names* the first facet. When you look at a diamond all the facets seem to be a slightly different colour but in reality they are all the same. As time goes on, you discover more and more of your facets and so your Purpose becomes *richer*. It does not tend to change, it just grows.

Your Purpose could be world-changing, or it could be life-changing on a local level; it doesn't really matter. There is no competition. The only question is: 'Is it important to *you*?' Gandhi's Purpose may have been 'the peaceful liberation of all people' and he put it into action in South Africa and India. Another person's Purpose may be geared towards how he or she gives themselves to their family and friends. There is no comparison you can draw; is a daffodil better than a rose? Your Purpose is *your* Purpose. The only thing that matters is that you live it to the full. That way your life becomes rich with meaning and you give your talents in such a way that it benefits your life and the lives of others. That is what makes a difference. You could live it as much through gardening as making peace in the Middle East.

Every human being has something special to offer, some unique contribution to make to the whole. You don't have the same teeth, eyes, voice, laugh, signature, fingerprints or smile as any other human being who has ever lived. Or who ever will live. You are as unique as every snowflake that has ever fallen: a perfect model of you. Not only that, but you have certain gifts, talents and abilities, many of which you have not yet used, or have lain dormant in you since childhood. You also have your life experience, which, of course, is distinctive from mine or anyone else's. That unique combination is like having a musical instrument that only you can play. It was designed by you, for you. Living your Purpose means picking it up and playing your heart out. As you do, others will start to pick up theirs and the orchestra of the world will sing rich and strong. The more of us who play our instruments the better life is. If you don't play, the world will keep on turning but your part of the orchestra will be silent. Are you really special? You are the only one there is and the only person who can live your best life. *And*, it does not happen by accident.

I have not written this book to tell you how to live your life. I couldn't do that with my integrity because I don't know about your life – I only know about mine. My job, and that of this book, is to help you find the most empowering, liberating and fulfilling ways you could live out your years on this planet. You already know everything you need to know. Your ticket to self-mastery is simply finding out what you know, naming it and using it. Your wisdom is complete. You may simply have never used it so directly before.

Purpose is the source of meaning and therefore of our true intent within; everything good starts there. As you move deeply into your truth, you become a powerful figure of integrity. Your communication becomes clearer and more direct. Your creativity becomes more pronounced and, because you start living for something greater than yourself, you vastly extend your collaborative abilities. In short, you become a more effective, dynamic and committed human being. People trust you more and you start to discover the extent of your abilities rather than being limited by your perception of them.

In living your Purpose, you evolve.

How to use this book

In two hours' time, if you follow this book through, you can have your Purpose. The process only takes a very short amount of time because the questions are asked to your creative/intuitive mind, which has little or no blocks. It is a quick and easy route into your deepest self. Because you already have all the answers you need, your Purpose will feel familiar and true to you, like an old friend.

Purpose

To find out what your Purpose is, you have to answer seven questions. First, each question is outlined, and then on the facing page you will find some tips to help you give your truest answer. The programme works best if you take it stage by stage; try not to skip any of these or jump ahead. I suggest you read the book with a notepad and a pencil handy so you are ready to answer these questions as you go through them.

Once you've answered these questions, you will be guided to writing your Purpose statement. This will define what your Purpose is to you.

When you know your Purpose we'll have a look at some examples of others who have gone through this process and what they have achieved by it, and we'll explore some of your own answers a little further. We'll also learn how to experience your Purpose in a number of different ways, so that it becomes a defining moment and enters into the fabric of your being.

Attitude

Once you have a clear understanding of what your Purpose is, we will look at how you can bring this most precious part of yourself to life through your behaviours. I call this section Attitude. Developing a Purposeful Attitude helps you develop changes in your behaviours that ensure your Purpose becomes a reality, bringing greater success, fulfilment and harmony to your life.

Again, there are some simple exercises you can do that will help you follow, stage by stage, the process to developing your own Attitude.

Means

If Purpose truly is the essence of fulfilment, it makes sense to help it grow and flourish.

Here, we will look at how to live your Purpose in every area of your life, every day of your life. This goal-setting, expressing our Purpose in the world we live in, I call the Means section of the programme. Again, there are some key tools to help your Purpose take root and prosper in the most helpful way. The Means section is built around using your creative intuition. I have always found creativity to be faster, more enjoyable and a more direct route than logic, and our intuition is simply the shortest distance between two points. Means consists of some simple exercises designed to engage the subconscious, intuitive and creative minds simultaneously. The result is a process that is unusual, imaginative and extraordinarily effective. To start with it will feel a bit like 'mind magic' but after a short while you will wonder how you ever lived without it.

Toolkit

Finally, I've included a 'toolkit' designed to help you cultivate the work you have done through the Purpose | Attitude | Means programme. These tools are different to the ones you've worked on in the book, because by then you will have completed the programme and be living your Purpose. As a result you will be living beyond the boundaries of your experience. Your life will become more refined and you will start to feel that 'extra lift'. The tools are a variety of 'in-flight enablers' to make the ride more comfortable and effective. They help you find the easy way to grow your Purpose.

The Purpose | Attitude | Means process was developed in a workshop environment. To help you understand what it is we are seeking to achieve in the sections of the book that require you to contemplate and note down your responses, I have included stories about people starting on their journey.

At some stage in your life you will want to know what your Purpose is, and when you do you will wonder why it took you so long to find out. If not now, when? And if not with me, then with whom and how?

PURPOSE

Confidence comes from great commitment
or great clarity.
Purpose gives you both.

The following process to help you find and name your Purpose consists of seven questions. *As there is no relationship between effort and effectiveness* it is a very simple process. Each question acts as a kind of search-engine for your imagination, setting your subconscious mind free to gather the information necessary to the naming and fundamental understanding of your Purpose.

The Yes Factor

There is a way to know whether or not any answer you give is completely satisfying to you, on all levels, and that is to see how much your answer says 'Yes' to you on a scale of 1-10. If your answer falls below an 8, I will help you move your answer up the scale. It is a simple and highly effective way to help you give and access the best of yourself. In the process, we only ever action answers which are an 8 or above on the 'Yes Factor' scale. It's a fundamental guiding principle for life; after all, why would you want to action a 6 when you could action a 9?

Your Purpose *is* the best of yourself. The Yes Factor helps you know and live it.

How do we move the number up the scale? If you were being invited out tonight and the person gives you the choice of going to the cinema or to a restaurant, which one would say 'Yes' to you most? If the cinema is a 9 out of 10 and the restaurant a 7, your decision is clear. If, however, you wanted to move your 7 to a 9, you might ask yourself, 'What restaurant says "Yes" to me 9 out of 10 tonight?' Your answer will be both satisfying and obvious. That's how simple the Yes Factor is. Your 8, 9 and 10 answers are the highest possibility you can conceive of for yourself. As we perform 8, 9 and 10 actions, we get 8, 9 and 10 results.

We will apply that process to the questions coming up. All you have to do is answer the questions honestly and openly, making sure that each answer you give says 'Yes' to you on a core level, 8, 9 or 10 out of 10. If it's an 8, 9 or 10 it's in. If it's not, it's not. You only want the best for yourself. Constructing your answer around your Yes Factor will give it to you.

Answering the Questions

Before you start, here are some guidelines to help you with this section of the process. After reading them you may find that you would like to take a moment to free your mind. Often listening to a piece of music that makes your mind wander helps. Simon and Garfunkel's 'If I could . . .' is a good example.

All at once?

My suggestion is to sit down and answer all the questions in one sitting. This typically takes an hour and a half to two hours – not a long time to discover your Purpose. Answering the questions all at once brings a momentum to our discovery and facilitates the process. Answering one question per week is a bit like going to the gym once a month; you get a work-out but you're not going to get fit.

If you cannot spare two hours, you really need to discover your Purpose! It will save you a lot of time. Give yourself the gift of a quiet morning or evening. If you have to wait two weeks that's fine; it's just another two weeks without your Purpose.

One at a time

This process speaks to your creative/intuitive mind, enabling you to find your most truthful responses effortlessly, regardless of how much your logical mind likes to block them. The questions are very specific and are designed to be answered in a particular order. Don't read ahead; it's counter-productive. If you look ahead, and then decide to go back and answer the questions, you will colour your answers and deprive yourself of the freshness spontaneity brings. Please read one question at a time and observe the special conditions of each. Some require you to answer in fewer than ten words, others ask you for seven suggestions. They are designed to help you get to clarity and to engage the richest part of your consciousness, and they work. Thousands of people have been through this process and what you are reading is the refinement of that work. Be completely honest in your answers as if nobody else will ever see what you have written. You cannot get the answers wrong.

Trust your answers

These core questions are asked in 'what if' scenarios. For example, 'What if you could do this . . . What if the world were like this, how would you be, what would you do?' The reason for this is that the logical mind puts up obstacles which obstruct us in the discovery of our greatest potential. This means that if I ask you, 'What's your Purpose?' most people cannot answer the question. It does not mean they do not know, only that the question is not helpful. Instead, therefore, we will approach the same question from the more fertile realms of the imagination, the golden bridge uniting the conscious and the subconscious. Most people are unfamiliar with the workings of their subconscious. That's okay. The questions ask you to give your intuitive response and then 'pop' them up the Yes Factor scale to an 8, 9 or even 10 out of 10. You have to *trust* what comes to you through your imagination and intuition. Listen to the first response that comes to you, even if it is accompanied by a little nagging voice telling you that it's not what you'd normally consider doing. As Nelson Mandela famously quoted Marianne Williamson: 'Our deepest fear is not that we are inadequate. Our deepest fear is that we are powerful beyond measure. It is our light, not our darkness that most frightens us.'

Facilitation tips

On the page facing the question are guidelines and tips to help you articulate your answers clearly and Purposefully. They help you move your answers up the Yes Factor scale, making sure that you get to an 8, 9 or 10, giving the best to yourself.

I recommend using the Facilitation questions after putting down your initial response and see if they change or enhance what you have done. Sometimes the tips are alternative ways of asking the same question, sometimes the phrasing of the question is reshaped to help you come to an intuitive response.

No examples

You will find that as we proceed with the questions I do not give examples of what others say or write in response with the exception of one instance. This is because we sometimes unconsciously say, 'That's the right way of doing something. So I'll give a similar answer.' However we are not interested in everybody else's Purpose at this stage, only in our own. We are all unique and our Purpose reflects this. Once we have completed the process we will look at examples of others.' For the moment we must have the courage to see the best in ourselves regardless of how we assume others may see us.

Honesty and integrity

Be honest, it will save you a lot of time and effort. Honesty is the cornerstone of integrity and the gateway to truth. Many people think that being honest is 'owning up to their bad points'. My experience is that people are far more loving, kind and giving than they give themselves credit for. Allow your honesty to shine your brightness and dissolve your obstacles. It will bring you to a greater truth in your answers.

Discovering the diamond

Some people get a bit jittery at this stage, just before they start answering the questions, asking things like, 'Do I have to commit to this Purpose for the rest of my life? Does this mean I can't change my mind later? This is a bit like deciding to marry someone I haven't yet met. How do I know that I am making the right choice for me?'

These are all good questions, but not really relevant to this stage of the process, as you'll see as we continue. Why? Because each question is designed to help you find the most meaningful answers from within. They come from *You*. So if you don't like the answers enough to commit to them, choose ones that you can commit to.

Our Purpose is like our spine. It is within us all the time in every action we perform and everywhere we go. Yet, if we sit still and try to 'feel' our spine, we can't do it. It doesn't mean that our spine isn't there, only that our awareness is not acute enough to feel it. Imagine now that your Purpose is that diamond locked deep within you. It, like our spine, resides within us, yet for some reason we have never felt it or identified it. This process is about uncovering the first facet of that diamond. The Purpose statement you will come out with at the end of the seven questions will name that first facet.

This is all in the future and doesn't really concern us now. For the time being, find a quiet place to be, sharpen the pencil, have a fresh, clean notebook in front of you and get into that Sunday-afternoon-squashy-armchair-comfortable-smell-of-hot-buttered-toast space and settle into some gentle humming contemplation.

Here goes . . .

THE SEVEN QUESTIONS

Question 1
part 1

Desert Island a

You and a number of others, enough to make up a small community, are stranded on a desert island. It is an 8, 9 or 10 out of 10 desert island, whatever that means to you. There is plenty of food, water and shelter and so survival is not a problem. The winds and tides dictate that you will have to stay here for a good amount of time, and the geography of the island is such that you have to live within the community.

1. How do you choose to *contribute actively* to that society?

2. How do you choose to *nourish yourself* in this environment?

Facilitation Tips

1. Imagine or write a paragraph describing your 8, 9 or 10 island.

2. Please answer the questions purely, without interpretation. Interpretation says things like: 'He probably means, what would I be likely to do?' The question is absolute. In the circumstances of the scenario, how do you choose to contribute actively to this society? Nothing else is the answer to this question.

3. List your answers; a maximum of six. When you feel complete, Yes Factor them, i.e., look at each suggestion and ask: 'How much does this say "Yes" to me out of 10?' Make sure that your answers say 'Yes' to you 8, 9 or 10 out of 10. If they don't, ask yourself, 'What could I do to contribute actively which would say "Yes" to me 8, 9 or 10 out of 10?' Or alternatively you could put the question like this: 'If I were to contribute actively in a way that says "Yes" to me 9 out of 10 I would probably do something like . . .'
Whatever comes to you in that moment is likely to be your 9 out of 10 suggestion. Trust your intuition.

4. 'How would you choose to nourish yourself?' This means, 'How do you choose to help and support yourself? In this situation what would you do to generate a quality of life that says "Yes" to you 8, 9 or 10 out of 10?'

5. Choose your top one to three answers depending on how many you have written down, and get ready to move on. We are not looking to draw any conclusions at this stage, only to answer the questions.

6. Finally, if there was such a thing as a 10 out of 10 response to the questions, they would be things like . . .

Write down your answers.

Question 1
part 2

Desert Island b

So . . . you build a raft to leave Desert Island a and the winds and tides eventually land you on the shores of a second island. If the first island was an 8, 9 or 10 out of 10 for you on your Yes Factor scale, this island is a 5, 6 or 7 out of 10, whatever that means to you. There is plenty of food, water and shelter for you so survival is not an issue. You have to stay on this island for a good amount of time until conditions change and the geography of the island dictates that you have to live in the community there.

1. How do you choose to *contribute actively* to the society?

2. How do you choose to *nourish yourself* in that environment?

Facilitation Tips

1. Imagine or write a paragraph describing your 5, 6 or 7 island. What are the differences between this island and our first one? What makes it more of a 5, 6 or 7 than an 8, 9 or 10 island?

2. As before, Yes Factor your answers. They must score 8, 9 or 10 out of 10. This can be measured both in terms of enjoyment and appropriateness, i.e. 'How appropriate does this answer feel out of 10?'

3. Your answers may be the same or different to the previous island.

4. If any of your answers are 7 or below try the following questions to help you 'pop' them up the scale:

   a.   What sort of things would you be doing to contribute actively and nourish yourself if you were on an 8? On a 9?

   b.   A 9 out of 10 answer feels like . . . looks like . . . would probably be something like . . .

   c.   What could you say with absolute 10 out of 10 certainty, I would do that?

5. Choose your top 1–3 answers depending on how many you have written down, and get ready to move on.

Question 1
part 3

Desert Island c

The day comes when you leave this island. You take your raft and head out to sea back towards the first island or beyond. The winds and tides have another plan, however, and you are washed up on the shores of a third desert island. If the last island was a 5, 6 or 7 out of 10, this one is definitely a 2, 3 or 4 out of 10, whatever that means to you. There is still plenty of food, water and shelter for you so survival is not an issue. You have to stay on this island for a good amount of time until the winds and tides change, and the geography of the island dictates that you have to live in the community there.

1. How do you choose to **contribute actively** to the society?

2. How do you choose to **nourish yourself** in that environment?

Facilitation Tips

1. Imagine or write a paragraph describing your 2, 3 or 4 desert island. What is it like? What circumstances or factors make this island different from the ones before? What's different?

2. Whatever restrictions are placed on you by this situation and/or environment, you are still required to make choices which are an 8, 9 or 10 on your Yes Factor, both in terms of appropriateness and satisfaction.

3. Your answers may be the same or different to the previous island.

4. Push yourself. Come up with at least three 9 out of 10 suggestions. What would you have to give in this environment? How could you give it?

5. Find fail-safe ways to nourish yourself.

6. If you were 8, 9 or 10 out of 10 successful in putting your plans into action, how would life be for you here? Yes Factor your answers.

7. If it were possible to have 10 out of 10 answers they would be things like . . .

Your answers to this question give you a strategy to live in the 10 zone even if the outside world does not support this.

Question 2

Tombstone

If there was one word that describes how you would most like to be remembered, which would be etched on to your tombstone for evermore, what would that word be?

Facilitation Tips

1. The question is very specific. It does not say, 'How am I likely to be remembered?' or 'How do I think people would describe me?' The only question to answer is: How would you *like* to be remembered?

2. Sometimes it can be hard to answer a question like this straight out. So here is a process to make things simpler, more enjoyable and more complete. Choose seven words that describe how you would like to be remembered and then Yes Factor them. In this instance, I am going to give you some examples: honourable, kind, noble, compassionate, giving, loving and generous.

3. If there is one word that stands out as being 'the one' choose that. It may be that you can't pick one out; in which case, here's a way to find that one word. Look at your list and see which words naturally go together. It is likely that among your seven words there are some with a similar meaning – like different facets of the same diamond. From the examples above, I would instinctively group together:

> *honourable and noble*
> *compassionate, loving and kind*
> *giving and generous*

This makes three separate groups. Now choose one word to represent each of those groups so that you end up with three words.

For example, honourable + noble = noble (for me nobility of character includes honour). However, I could also put 'honest' down as this speaks to me in the same way. You need to make a personal choice. Compassionate + loving = loving (for me 'loving' necessarily includes compassion and kindness, especially in its 8, 9 or 10 out of 10 form).

Compassionate + loving + kind = loving.

The next step is to try to merge your three words to get one that says 'Yes' to you 9 or 10 out of 10. See what the qualities suggest to you. Sometimes they are obvious, sometimes surprising and delightful. This is a wonderful exercise and well worth remembering for other situations. Sometimes people get cold feet about how beautiful and moving their words are, how much they mean to us personally and of the implications they might hold. It's okay: you don't have to show this to anyone, it's just for you. Write down the word that is true for you in spite of any cynicism or internal criticism you may encounter: leave that outside the door. Cynicism is not truth.

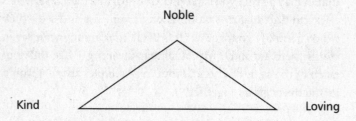

Noble

Kind

Loving

So, noble + kind might = ? True.

True + loving might = ? True or Truthful.

In another example the three words blended together were: knightly, generous and kind. The resultant word that went on the tombstone was 'Shepherd'. Sometimes other words hold a stronger meaning for us. Trust what says 'Yes' to you most. Keep to one word and try to make it one used in language as opposed to making it up. Remember: Nobody has a monopoly on truth. My answers as the merged qualities of different words are the answers that are true for me. You must determine what answers you would give that are true to you.

4. Then ask: 'How happy would I be if this were etched on to my tombstone after my death?' If my answer is 9 or 10 out of 10 this question is complete. If not, an 8 might be something like . . .

   A 9 would be more like . . .

   The perfect 10 out of 10 answer, if it were possible, would be something like . . .

5. You can test the word out for yourself by running it through your head: 'Here lies [my name], "True". Rest In Peace'.

   Write down your final word in a little RIP tombstone sketch.

6. Some have a concern at this point, wondering if they are arrogant to attribute such wonderful qualities to themselves. This process is about determining what your values and aspirations are. By choosing a word you are not saying, 'This is the way I am all of the time, or even most of the time,' you are simply saying, 'This word stands for something which is 9 or 10 out of 10 important to me. I would love this word to be a constant theme in my life.'

7. Make sure you have one word that speaks to you 8, 9 or 10 out of 10 before moving on to answer the next question.

Question 3

The Book of Life

Imagine there is a Book of Life in which each person has one paragraph, consisting of three sentences, describing what they *gave* in this lifetime.

What would you like your entry to say?

1. Each sentence must be fewer than fifteen words.

2. They must say 'Yes' to you deeply, 8, 9 or 10 out of 10.

3. Be as specific as you can.

Facilitation Tips

1. Imagine your entry is written at the end of your long and fulfilling life and that it sums up your three major contributions.

2. Restricting your answers to fewer than fifteen words helps you get to clarity. Clarity is a key to self-confidence and self-knowledge.

3. Yes Factor yourself on how clean and well defined your entry is. Be as specific as you can. Generalisation will not get you where you want to go.

4. When you have completed your entry, look to see if you are saying essentially the same thing in two or more of the sentences. If so, how would the sentences read were you to combine them?

5. If you have written your sentences in fewer than fifteen words, how few words can you use to write your entry with the same or greater impact? Try using five words; it will get you to the essence of what you want to give.

6. Hard to answer? Try this:

   Imagine it is at least 100 years into the future. You are a disembodied spirit hanging around the pearly gates of heaven and you see the Archangel Gabriel talking to the book-keeper and a number of other saints. You glance over their shoulders and, lo and behold, your name is at the top of the page, with three sentences underneath describing what you gave.

   They read . . .

   1)

   2)

   3)

Question 4

Song Slogan

Imagine for a moment that there were another part of you, a light-shadow, if you like, that went with you everywhere. It can speak, sing, move and dance but is invisible and inaudible to others. It can only be seen and heard by the light-shadows of other people. Now, imagine that it were to sing out a song-slogan to the world at the top of its voice, 24 hours a day, 7 days a week, 365/6 days per year.

What would you like your song-slogan to be?

Facilitation Tips

1. A song-slogan is a short message or phrase that means something to you. It could be from a song you already know, if that says 'Yes' to you 10 out of 10, or you can make one up.

2. Your song-slogan must say 'Yes' to you 8, 9 or 10 out of 10. If you are going to hear it somewhere in your being 24 hours per day, 7 days a week, you may as well make it a 9 or 10 out of 10 slogan.

3. If you're struggling with this one: imagine you loved life, were passionate about the world in a sunshiny way and that if you had to sing a song-slogan (maximum five words) expressing your state or giving a simple message to be sung out to the world, you would sing something like . . .

4. How much does your answer say 'Yes' to you out of 10?

Question 5

World Microphone

Imagine . . .

The world microphone is a device that broadcasts on every piece of media on the planet simultaneously – every television and radio station, cinema screen, website, newspaper, magazine, book, newsletter; everything, all at the same time.

In a short while, you will have sole use of the world microphone for fifteen minutes. How do you use your time? What is your message? Write a sentence, a paragraph, or a page to describe what you would say. Your answer must say 'Yes' to you on a core level, 9 or 10 out of 10.

Facilitation Tips

1. Make the situation real for yourself. If you really had access to such a tool, what would you want to do with it? What is the best use you can make of it? And what is your core message?
2. What does your answer tell you is so important to you that you would use your fifteen minutes of fame in this way?
3. If you can write an 8 or 9 out of 10 answer, what is a 10?
4. An alternative question for those who imagine themselves afraid of public speaking: If somehow you could intravenously drip a message into the ear of every person on the planet while they slept, what would it be?

Question 6
part 1

Super-heroes

If you were a super-hero, what seven powers would you most like to have?

1.
2.
3.
4.
5.
6.
7.

What would your name as a super-hero be?

Facilitation Tips

1. You can have established super-hero powers such as flying and breathing underwater and ones that you make up for yourself. There is no limit to what you can have. You decide.

2. Yes Factor each answer. Only put down ones that truly say 'Yes' to you 8, 9 or 10 out of 10.

3. Make sure you complete this section, putting down all seven powers.

4. Please do not turn over the page until you have completed this section.

Question 6
part 2

This question does not make sense. Please answer it anyway.

If, in two weeks' time, you wake up in the morning and discover you have one of the seven powers you wrote down, *which one is it most likely to be?*

Facilitation Tips

1. People are often puzzled by this part of the question and try to answer the question, 'Which power would I most like it to be?' That is not the question. The question is which one is it most *likely* to be. Whether that makes sense or not, please answer it. We will find out why later.

Question 6
part 3

In two weeks' time you wake up in the morning and discover that you have this power.

Realistically, what do you do with it?

Facilitation Tips

1. Your answer must say 'Yes' to you 9 or 10 out of 10.
2. Imagine really waking up in the morning and having this power or ability. How do you choose to use it for the greater good? If it's not for the greater good, are you really a hero?
3. If you have an 8 out of 10 answer, a 9 would be more like . . .
4. What's the best use you can imagine for this power? What could give you most satisfaction and fulfilment in its use? How would life be if this were true and you really followed through? What would your life in the modern world be like?

Question 7

Purpose Statement

Digesting all that you have written and considered, complete the following sentence using ten words or fewer, in a way that says 'Yes' to you 9 or 10 out of 10.

I serve the Purpose of . . .

Facilitation Tips

1. Please keep the phrasing of the sentence. Sometimes people like to change it to 'My Purpose is . . .' This is less powerful and active. Your Purpose necessarily must be larger than you, i.e. something you serve, and active. 'I serve the Purpose of' implies both.

2. Make it a Yes Factor of 9 out of 10 . . . you know the drill.

3. Make it clean, solid and complete. If what you have written is true for you, it will feel powerful and have an expansive quality: in other words the more you think about it the more implications it has.

4. If you can complete the sentence using only two, three or five words, what would they be? I suggest writing the longer version first and then refine it down. Yes Factor your short version. Does it feel more complete and powerful than the original?

5. Imagine living true to this Purpose every day of your life. How fulfilled would you feel? How might your life be different in five years' time?

6. Your Purpose statement does not have to mean anything to anyone else. It is only for you. It is more about *being* it than *telling* it.

7. Is it likely to be meaningful to you in six months' time? How about in a year?

8. What Purpose can you truly serve 10 out of 10?

I suggest putting the book down and having a break before reading on.

Well done.

Using the Seven Questions

You have now named your Purpose. When you look at it and read the sentence through to yourself, it should feel true to who you are, as if it were something you always knew but had never named.

The following sections are designed to deepen your experience of it, so that the words come off the page and into your emotional reality.

Looking back over some of the answers you gave to the seven questions, there is probably a lot that you would like to know more about. All the answers you wrote deal with you, your values and priorities. Now, let's revisit them and look at a few stories from other people, to get an idea of their Purpose statements, and what their answers to the questions meant to them. As you read them you may wish to revisit your answers to delve deeper into your insight and understanding.

1> Desert Islands

Jeff is a successful international lawyer and a caring family man. He is someone you feel you can implicitly trust. As well a having a flourishing career, Jeff is a talented and prolific artist. Not only does he paint with the sophistication and flair of a skilled artist, he also speaks and expresses himself passionately in that way. He is most definitely an artist and a lawyer. Both sides of his character are expressed in these activities, yet not completely so. To some extent he had followed in his father's footsteps in becoming a lawyer and art was his great love. At the back of his mind there had always been the nagging questions: Was he really an artist or a lawyer? Was he living his truest life or had he settled for something less?

He undertook the seven questions, not because he felt that his life lacked meaning, but because he wished to move to another level of integrity, where all his gifts and talents would unite and lift him to the next stage of his evolution.

When he had completed the desert islands set of questions, he knew. His choices in all three islands were the same: he chose to help those less fortunate than himself using all his gifts to serve those ends. Bringing in *all* his talents necessarily meant combining his artistic abilities with those of an acute and structured mind. He completed the remaining questions but in actual fact his dilemma was already resolved. His Purpose statement reads:

I serve the Purpose of Growing Artistic Living.

No longer would his artistic life be secondary to his professional one. He chose to express it in his work, his family life, in his relationships, his sport and health and in his paintings. This new unity of Purpose brought his talents together and gave rise to a profound letting go. He is more settled and secure within himself and his abilities have deepened.

Sathya Sai Baba says, 'Either love what you do, or do what you love.' Either way it will bring us to the same point: love. It is the expression of all our greatest gifts. In Jeff's case as in mine and many others', Purpose allows us to bring the whole of ourselves to all of life and the best of us grows.

A desert island is a place where we can be truly free. Free from social pressures, distractions of the modern world and even responsibilities, if we choose. Our needs are minimal and because having food, water and shelter is a given, we are free to make the choices that say 'Yes' to us most.

Whatever you chose, then, is what you would choose if you were free. And, the good news is, you are free. So if you simply start to action those choices in an intelligent way, you will be living your 8, 9 or 10 life.

Looking back over your answers:

- What do you notice about your responses to the first part of the question: how do you choose to contribute actively to that environment?
- Are there any similarities and constant themes that show up? Are they different or the same? What do your answers tell you?

How about your choices about nourishing yourself?

If we are giving according to our gifts in harmony with the whole and at the same time nourishing ourselves, we can make sure that we are in a state of expansion not sacrifice.

In knowing how, from a place of freedom, we would choose to nourish ourselves, we get to understand what warms our heart and is integral to our being. Engaging in these activities helps us in every area of our life. It is likely that we are already doing these things; however, many of us get caught up in a hailstorm of distractions buried beneath in-trays of 'must do's'. We forget to give to ourselves, which doesn't help us give our best. If we are giving to others 8, 9 or 10 out of 10 and giving to ourselves 2, 3 or 4 out of 10 we will burn out pretty quick. We have to put fuel in our car to give others a lift home.

- Were your answers different or similar in all three scenarios?
- What did you choose to do to nourish yourself throughout the spectrum of islands?
- Are you doing these things now?

If not, free choice has shown you this is how you like to generate your well-being. You now have a strategy to nourish yourself if you choose it.

- Which environment speaks loudest to you of your current situation in life?
- What helpful ways of dealing with these situations did you identify in the island scenarios that you could apply now?
- What constitutes a 2, 3 or 4 and a 5, 6 or 7 environment? Are there any similarities?

Your answers to these questions show you how you would find the greatest happiness for yourself and give the best you have to offer no matter how inhospitable the outside world is.

If you answered the questions with an 8, 9 or 10 Yes Factor, it proves that your imagination can furnish you with enlightened choices in all situations. It's like having a universal 'get out of jail free' card.

**If you can generate 8, 9 or 10 experiences
in a 2, 3 or 4 environment,
you are free.**

2 > Tombstone

Tombstone is a very important question. It literally asks us to decide what values and qualities mean most to us. When we know what our true values are we know how we want to be in this life. It is so easy to get distracted with work, money and trivial details, but as the famous quote says 'Who, on their death-bed, ever said, "I wish I'd spent more time in the office?"' or, for that matter, 'surrounded by their bank statements'?

Elizabeth is an attractive, well-meaning and thoughtful woman. She grew up in an environment where it was 'uncool' to be caring. People who genuinely wanted the best for others were seen as 'soft' or as 'having ideas above their station'. Such attitudes can make Purposeful living hard to sustain. When she came to answer this question she was confronted by two sides to herself. On the one hand she could put down the seven words she felt would be most acceptable to others, while on the other she could put down the words that carried the most weight and meaning for her personally. Ultimately, in the sorting process, she had to pare her words down to three and then two. These were: 'genuine' and 'beautiful'. 'Genuine', or authentic, was how she wished to be with others and 'beautiful' was the inner quality she wished to radiate. Because of her environment and role models she found it hard to bring these two qualities together. She had no role models who shone with both these fine qualities. Being a woman who is used to being seen as attractive, she had dedicated more of her behaviours to her appearance which was more socially acceptable than her values. The tombstone process asks people to unite their favourite qualities not to choose between them. In her mind, therefore, she started to picture a possibility for herself where she could be both 'genuine' and 'beautiful'. She chose 'beautiful' as being the term that most spoke to her of both qualities, and, by the end of the question, she had begun the process of becoming her own role model.

Her Purpose statement is:

I serve the Purpose of making a difference in people's lives for the greater good of the world.

Elizabeth had been an aerobics instructor as well as working in a business context. She then decided to become a personal development facilitator. Within a year of naming her Purpose she was facilitating groups at the highest level.

Susan was educated by nuns, had had a successful career in PR and was now bringing up two young children, whom she adored. She had no trouble writing down her seven words. She was clear what they stood for and how much they meant to her. However, when she came to finding one word that spoke of the qualities of

- Love
- Kindness
- Compassion
- Giving
- Care
- Inspiration
- Generosity

All she could think of were words that held a profound spiritual significance for her, such as 'saintly', 'Christian', 'angelic,' which she found hard to accept. Could she allow herself to think about herself in such a way? Much of her childhood education had left such violent and negative religious impressions for her, that if she were to choose any of those words, guilt was surely attached in some way. Could she really live up to these aspirations or would she be punished for thinking so? As we examined these questions together it became clear that these were the values she genuinely found to be the most spectacular and beautiful she could imagine and that she did not have to be them all the time. The exercise had shown her what she wished to cultivate and grow inside herself. She knew that the character of her children was not created or set in a single moment, but grows day by day; in the same way her chosen tombstone quality, 'Christian', would grow and extend each day that she championed it. Moreover she began to see that there was a real difference between the *experience* of Christianity for her and the meaning she associated with it from her education.

Choosing 'Christian' as her tombstone quality allowed her to have a new and personal relationship to God, unfettered by guilt and duty. She had set herself free.

The words we choose to describe how we would like to be remembered describe what is fundamentally important to us: our values. Everything else is largely unimportant.

I have never heard anyone when asked, 'What word would you like etched on your tombstone for evermore to describe you?' answer 'arrogant', 'overbearing', 'controlling', 'slim', 'timid', 'flashy' or 'powerful'. Yet these words and others like them can describe our behaviour day in and day out. If this is so, we are living out of balance with our values and that can only mean a life filled with regrets when the death-bed time comes.

So, if you would like to be remembered in a particular way why wait until you are on your death-bed to start thinking about it? You could do that thinking now, cut out a lot of wasted time and start to become those values. Then, your wishes come true.

- If there were any other words you could add to your list so that it felt more complete what would they be?
- How could you be more of these words on a day-to-day basis?
- How do you think your life would improve?

**The seven words you have chosen
represent your values;
the more you live them,
the more Value-able you are.**

3 › The Book of Life

*Days are like scrolls. Write on them what you
want remembered.*
The Talmud

Dave, like many of us, had hopes and dreams. If he had
been in a fairytale, he would have been one of those
people who 'went off to seek their fortune'. His ambitions
always took him to somewhere or something new. He
changed jobs and relationships often and seemed more
preoccupied with having a 'lifestyle' than a full and rich
life. The difficulty he encountered with such various and
burning ambitions was that:

a) He found it hard to settle long enough in one
endeavour to make any real headway; like the person
who wants to dig a drinking well but who constantly
changes their mind after digging a couple of feet about
where the well should be located and so never goes
deep enough to find a nourishing source.

b) He was somehow waiting for the world to discover
him. He had great ideas and aspirations and felt that
one day something miraculous would happen and he
would somehow be propelled into the limelight. This
belief meant that he was living a constant waiting
game. His dreams had not yet happened to him and
this gave rise to frustration and resentment in him.

The Book of Life asks us to define ourselves by what we *give*, not by what we *get*. When Dave articulated his dreams from this perspective, he realised that they were, in fact, very practical and therefore well within his grasp; it was up to him to make them happen. His dreams were merely his blueprint; it was his actions that determined whether or not they came true. Many of us know this mentally, but how many of us *become* this understanding?

Dave also looked at what said 'Yes' to him 9 or 10 out of 10. His answers were very down to earth. Having been a bit of a philanderer, he was surprised that what he wanted to give was to create and cherish a healthy, loving and caring family. He knew that this was true for him. He also knew that some of his habits made this very difficult to realise.

The result was that he stopped waiting and began to take an active role in creating his future. He became responsible for his actions. He has grown in success in his field and he and his wife are awaiting their first child.

The Book of Life asks you to make the life-shopping list from the point of view of giving rather than getting. It asks you to do it clearly and concisely and to be committed to your answers. What contribution would you like to make to the planet? How would you like the world to be richer as a result of your having been a part of it? These questions are simple and very deep. Placing these questions into the context of a Book of Life helps us to focus our intentions around a single point. Allowing an element of imagination encourages us to bring our whole selves to the answer and express that intent completely.

Now that you know . . .

- Is there any way you could give yourself more to the areas you identified in your answers to this question?
- What changes would you have to make to live your answers?

**The Book of Life says 'you live what you give'.
What do you truly want?**

4> Song Slogan

A song does not have to make sense. It could say 'imagine all the people living life in peace' or 'wop-bop-alubop-a-wop-bam-boom'. They both express perfectly what the writer felt when writing. The same is true for the song-slogan. In this question there is nothing to get right and nothing to prove. For many of us this releases both creativity and authenticity. Also, the previous questions have been, for the most part, personal. Now, for the first time in the process you are asked to consider what you would profoundly like to express *to others*.

People often give more consideration to others than they do to themselves. When Jonathan undertook the seven questions he took a week to write his answer to this question. It was worth the wait:

> *Watch your thoughts; they become words.*
> *Watch your words; they become actions.*
> *Watch your actions; they become habits.*
> *Watch your habits; they become your character.*
> *Watch your character; it becomes your destiny.*

The wisdom and clarity he gave birth to through the question have become guiding principles for him in his life. Jesus had key guiding principles: 'Do unto others as you would have them do unto you,' 'Love thy neighbour as thyself' and 'Turn the other cheek,' as did Gandhi: 'We must become the changes we seek in the world,' as did Mohammed, Buddha, Moses, Lao Tse, Winston Churchill, my father, my friends and probably yours too. The guiding principles we keep, define who we become and the quality of our actions.

Most of what we write down is common sense. *What changes our life is when our common sense becomes our common practice.* For Jonathan, as for many others, the song-slogan helped him articulate his guiding principles clearly. Practising them has helped him become a more responsible, clearer-thinking, empowered and confident human being. He has evolved.

Jonathan's Purpose statement is:

I serve the Purpose of Natural Justice.

There is a very strong connection with this Purpose and the natural quality of cause and effect articulated through his song-slogan.

Most people like to sing. They sing when they are happy. What, therefore, would they be happy to sing forevermore? If we were to have one message that we would hear somewhere inside ourselves 24 hours per day, 365 days per year, we would really have to like it. What says 'Yes' to us that much?

The questions, until this point, have dealt with your conscious choices: what would you choose to do from a point of freedom and what is most important to you. For the first time, now we enter into your emotional life. For the emotions to speak to us and inform us of their 8, 9 or 10 choice they need a language. Music, colour, texture and taste are those languages. Of these music is the most generic and the easiest to associate with words and a message. In answering this question you are delving into your emotional possibilities and seeing what it says.

Not only will your answer tell you what is 8, 9 or 10 out of 10 important to you, it will give you a direct connection with that feeling, probably for the rest of your life. Often the subconscious mind will make suggestions to us in the form of music and lyrics. As these are often played in the background to our more conscious thoughts, many people forget to listen to them. Listen to the jukebox from time to time and see what it's suggesting.

- If everyone in the world were to hear your song-slogan, what positive message would it send out?
- Is this, perhaps, what you really think and feel, whether or not you show it?
- What if you were to become an example of this message, what would that be like?

What's your core message?
How do you want people to feel when you walk out of the room?

5› World Microphone

People often remark after answering the seven questions that they never thought of themselves as *deep* before. More often than not they realise that this is because they have never been asked to consider anything more profound than the day-to-day details of life. The world microphone question, however, asks us to articulate what we consider to be most important in a clear and concise way. The fact that our communication will appear on every piece of media on the planet encourages us to write our message in a way that others will understand. That way we do not complicate things; rather, we keep them simple. When people articulate meaningful things simply, they go very deep.

Rachel found herself declaiming her world microphone message. Its profound nature took her by surprise, so much so that she dismissed it at first as being 'silly'. Only later when she shared it with her husband and others did she come to realise that it was exactly what she felt and probably exactly what the world needs to hear. Here's what she said:

> *People of this earth, you might think we are all so different; you might have feuds with your neighbours. You might think your way is the right way . . . But please, step back. Think! What is your Purpose?*
>
> *Surely, to have a great time whilst you live on Earth?*

*In that case **we all have the same purpose**. Surely if we all work together we can make sure each of us creates a happy, healthy environment. All we have to do is give our best in what we know and respect the work of others. Be open-minded and learn from others, just as you can teach them.*

Have faith but only in the truth! The truth is religion doesn't matter. God exists whether you call him Jesus, Allah, the Big Bang theory or the Sun.

The truth is we will never have a planet where everyone agrees with each other. However, we can agree to accept each others' different opinions just as we have friends of different religions, culture and ideology.

The truth is that only by questioning ourselves constantly do we become aware of all this and work towards bettering ourselves.

Take some time out and think about the truth. Only then will we be a team.

Rachel grew up in a country where people of different religious faiths persecuted others. She also had a tendency to become highly stressed about certain events in her life. Her message showed her both the strength of her commitment to tolerance *and* served as a reminder to her to enjoy life, not to take it all too seriously.

Her Purpose statement is:

I serve the Purpose of endless adventure.

The world microphone is a metaphor for impact and influence; as you grow into your Purpose, you become a more effective human being, no longer dissipating your energies any more. You inevitably have a greater impact and influence on those around you. What do you choose to dedicate that to?

When you live your Purpose you live for what is important and nothing else. This makes you much more effective in anything you do. This is often recognised by those around you. You may become an inspiration to them. You may even become famous. How will you use that fame or influence? Will you let it serve your Purpose?

Fame or recognition may become an inevitable part of your Purposeful journey. There is a big HOWEVER, though. If fame is the motivating factor for you, you will not be living for something greater than yourself, and thus not living your Purpose. You have to be clean.

This question is also important in terms of where it occurs in the process. For the first time you are being asked: What do you stand for? The world microphone is, to some, a great opportunity to say and give something meaningful to the world. For others it is a frightening prospect, asking them to commit strongly to beliefs while also asking what is more important to them than any fear of speaking to a huge audience. The effect of the scenario, therefore, helps us dig deep. We tend only to choose to say things that are truly important to us. Our messages are often the expression of values that are respected throughout all cultures and ways of life, which is the essence of our humanity.

The question is sandwiched between the song-slogan, which taps into your emotional life, and super-heroes, which asks you about your hidden gifts and talents. Imbued with an emotional richness from the previous question our answer joins the 8, 9 or 10 places of our head and our heart. What we say is true for us. So much so that it is this quality of truth that gives us the courage to speak to the world. This place, this integrity, this quality of commitment to personal truth is what sets us apart from purpose-less people and moves us on from our old life. Such a fearless quality is intoxicating and magnetic. It makes us stand out in our society, and that encourages fame and renown.

- What if you were a superstar or a powerful political leader, how would you use your influence?
- What if it lasted longer and you went past the point where you revelled in the attention and fortune? What would you like to do with the opportunity such attention affords you?

What means more to you than the trappings of success or more important to you than any fear?

6〉 Super-Heroes

When Alan answered the second part of the question, 'If you were to wake up in the morning in two weeks' time with one of these powers, which one is it most likely to be?' the power that jumped out at him from his list was 'the power to be loved by all'. He was reluctant to share this at first, feeling that the power he had chosen was a reaction to not feeling loved or appreciated. When we examined the answer to the last part of the question, 'Realistically, what do you do with that power?' he gave a wonderful description about empowering others to believe in themselves and go beyond their limits. In other words, he wanted to be valuable to the whole through having given of his Purpose.

Alan's Purpose statement was:

I serve the Purpose of enabling others to fly.

Whether or not Alan had chosen the power to be loved by all out of insecurity or compassion is irrelevant. It is what he chose to do with the gift that mattered. Many people are fabulously talented behind closed doors. Others may be less talented but give it all in the public arena and are recognised for it. How we choose to give is the only thing that matters.

The penny dropped for Jenny when she answered the super-heroes question. The first super-power she listed was the ability to change people's minds for their benefit. She instinctively felt that she did not need any other powers if this was possible since it would allow her to achieve everything she wished. She put down six other powers just for her own enjoyment. In parts 2 and 3 of the question where she was asked which power she was most likely to possess and what she would realistically do with it, she was again drawn to the original ability: to change people's minds from the inside – to their benefit. She understood that what she really wanted to do with her life was to make a difference. There were many ways she could help achieve this; given a free choice, however, she chose to help people address limiting attitudes and mindsets.

Jenny had taught sport for years. She has since begun training to be a facilitator and life-coach. Her Purpose statement is: I Serve the Purpose of making a difference.

So many people in modern society suffer from low self-esteem that it is practically an epidemic. It is said that when growing up, we hear an average of seventeen 'no's' to every 'yes'.

Like this, for example: 'No. No. No. No. No. No. No. Stop that. Not now. Don't. Enough! No. No. No. No more. No. No . . . er, okay go on then. No. No. No.'

Does that sound familiar? Obviously 'no' is appropriate some of the time; however, when it becomes so over-bearing it can leave scars. People who grow up with little or no confidence in their abilities and talents start to lose them. The talents are still there but because they don't believe in them any more they stop indulging in them.

If, for example, you were a good swimmer, but lost confidence in your ability, would you dive into the sea on a rough day and be invigorated by its life-giving energy? Or would you rather sit on the beach, throw stones and watch the surf breaking? Many people lose confidence in their abilities and so prefer to watch others enjoying theirs rather than participating and enriching the tapestry of life through giving themselves.

The super-heroes question is a response to that. It starts to redress the balance by asking ourselves, possibly for the first time, 'What would I be like if I were an unlimited being?' It places us in a situation where anything is possible and where we *allow ourselves* to have any talents we choose. The ones we choose, therefore, are important to us.

We often choose to have powers that are very close to our natural abilities; for example a person choosing 'telepathy' as a power may already be highly empathic, but may not fully trust their ability. Classic powers such as 'flying' and 'breathing underwater' often speak of a spirit of freedom which wishes to be expressed more in life.

Alongside a smattering of classic powers, participants to this process usually invent some of their own abilities such as kindness and love rays, emotional healing powers and the ability to change the fortunes of the world through affecting the environment or people's minds. The ability to stop war is a common theme.

The structure of the question asks us to draw answers

from the realm of infinite possibility and apply them in the realm of actuality. Since the ideas of super-heroes and super-powers are more acceptable to the subconscious mind than the conscious, it is the subconscious that answers the question. Its character does not give it the same level of discernment as the conscious mind, neither does it block possibilities such as hidden talents. This means that when it is asked about the power it is 'most likely' to have it chooses the one closest to its understanding. Frequently this is an extension of an ability we already have, or brings to the surface one that has been obscured through years of 'reasonable' adult thinking.

When asked what we would *realistically* do with the power we are most likely to accrue the question is again focusing our intent. Focused positive intent is the playground of our Purpose. Moreover, in answering the question we begin to imagine ourselves as actually having this power. This imagination, in itself, starts to draw the latent ability closer to the surface. I call this process of using the imagination to bring tangible results from the subconscious to the conscious 'imaginacting'. In answering the question as it stands we begin the process of imaginacting new abilities . . . We literally start to become a higher possibility of ourselves. This helps to complete the process, allowing our answers to the previous five questions to sink in and giving the space to allow us to answer the seventh question: our Purpose statement.

Have you ever wondered if you had some special gifts

or abilities? My experience of living on Purpose is that the moment we begin to live for something greater than ourselves we literally 'expand' our capabilities. Things we thought we simply could not do, we can or learn. Take Gandhi for example. When he began his work, he was in South Africa, standing up to the authorities through non-violent non-cooperation. What he was proposing was a radical departure from any other form of protest ever seen before. It was vitally important that he could communicate this effectively to those concerned. He had a great mind, and a spectacular heart but was a poor public speaker. His modest character did not naturally suit the limelight. However, he had a Purpose, which we might call 'the peaceful liberation of all people', that drove him beyond himself so he made sure that he learned and developed his speaking abilities to serve this Purpose better. The fact that India is no longer ruled by Britain is a testament to his success.

Again, this question is asking the same as the others. It says, 'You are special. There is nobody else quite like you in the world both in terms of your personality and your gifts. What would you most like to do with what you have?' Your particular brand of giving is your Purpose.

Out of the powers you chose, there are likely to be several that are simply extensions of normal abilities. Some may be great athletic prowess; others more attuned to the inner arts. A remarkable amount of people answer this question with gifts and powers relating to healing, intuition, telepathy, love and prosperity. Many, if not all, of us have these capabilities. It is my experience that capabilities are like a tooth waiting for a space to come through. We often need to have a cause for the talent to grow. Purpose is the cause.

- What if these capabilities were yours, how could you foster and nurture them?
- How would your life be enhanced by their use?
- How could they best serve your Purpose?

**Some achieve a great deal with very little.
Some achieve very little with a great deal.
What's the best you can achieve with
what you have?**

7 › I Serve the Purpose of . . .

Purpose is your essence and meaning expressed in the world. Knowing it and living it is the most important thing you can do in this lifetime. It brings happiness and fulfilment and it enriches the world. When people arrive at their Purpose statements they tend to feel as if they have landed or come home. It is as if they are now being called by an ancient name they once had and they know themselves anew.

Many also want to know how the Purpose statement they've written fits in with those of others, so below are some examples for you.

A client of mine, Rob, is the CEO of a large company. The Purpose statement he arrived at was:

I serve the Purpose of Christianity in action.

Obviously this spoke to him on many levels; he had no intention of foisting his spiritual beliefs and practices on others, so how would it affect the running of his business?

In the year following the discovery of his Purpose he has replaced rules and regulations with a values-based system of management. This means that giving, respect, trust, listening and kindness now typify the nature of all his company's business practices. He has also introduced training to develop all staff regardless of whether or not they are fee earners for the firm. A man Rob works with suffered a bereavement which affected his work and relationship with clients. Through working with his Purpose, Rob chose to adopt a very supportive, compassionate way of dealing with the situation even though it could have proved risky, financially. It worked out very well for him, and both the colleague and the business are going from strength to strength. Rob feels that he is doing things 'right' now. He feels as if he is being himself more than working to become 'correct' in the eyes of others. His horizons have expanded, he spends more quality time with his family and he has blossomed as an individual.

Sometimes the effects our Purpose statements will have on our life are not obvious at first. For example I took James, an actor, through the seven questions. The Purpose he arrived at spoke of his commitment to love and give to his friends and family. It touched him deeply and he knew that it was a true and driving force in his life. Over the following year he began to make significant changes in the direction of his career. He started his own theatre company and began running workshops using theatre to help young people learn and develop. He has proved an absolute natural and loves what he gives and gets from this new venture. It has brought him stability, success and meaning. The venture is not a literal translation of his Purpose in life; however, it is the manifestation of the same quality and values. Once he had discovered the 'flavour' of meaning through his Purpose statement, he could not settle for anything less elsewhere. This has led him to express his talents where they are most meaningful. Two years ago he was an actor. Now he directs, writes, produces and delivers training programmes. He is an inspiration to those around him and an amazement to his family and friends.

Welcome to the Purposeful group of people of which you are now a part.

I am Peter.
I serve the Purpose of inspiring evolution.

I am Linda.
I serve the Purpose of passionate joy.

I am Richard.
I serve the Purpose of marking and sharing the road to happiness.

I am Vana.
I serve the Purpose of compassionately serving.

I am Martin.
I serve the Purpose of being truth.

I am Susie.
I serve the Purpose of enabling awesome consciousness.

I am Belinda.
I serve the Purpose of radiating and celebrating the power of being.

I am Valerie.
I serve the Purpose of enabling the growth of humanity.

The rest of this book is dedicated to helping you become a living, breathing expression of your statement.

Experiencing Your Purpose

Now we can do more to understand our Purpose; you have written out your Purpose statement, but is that enough? The following suggestions are ways of developing your understanding of your Purpose. In the Means section of the book we will look at ways of setting and achieving goals and creating long-term Purpose-driven movements in every area of our lives. However, for the moment, anything that engages you with your Purpose, either on a metaphorical or direct level, makes it more tangible in your life. It starts to drive your actions and helps you become 'Purpose fit'. These simple exercises help you engage with and *feel* your Purpose, on a number of different levels. That way, when you develop your Attitude, your Purpose becomes an expression of *all* of you, and not just an idea. Doing these simple exercises gives a fuller understanding of what our Purpose is in a way that we cannot get intellectually.

There are no right or wrong answers in the following questions, just pop down your immediate response, and see where it leads you. It's good fun, and helps to deepen your experience of your Purpose, so that the words come off the page and into your emotional reality. You don't have to do anything with your answers. They are there to give you a fuller, more definite feeling of the character of your Purpose. Some of them require you to jot something down on paper;

some of them only ask you to think about the question. Do as many or as few as you like – whatever say 'Yes' to you on an 8, 9 or 10 . . .

1. If your Purpose was a:

    Meal, *Taste* or *Flavour*, it would probably be something like . . .

    Picture, it would probably be . . .

    Colour, it would be something like . . .

    Place, it would be . . .

    Sound . . .

    Song, or *piece of music* . . .

    Smell . . .

2. What moments in films/books/articles/stories does it remind you of?

3. What person alive, dead or fictitious does it remind you of?

4. Where do you feel it in your body? How does it feel? Describe the sensation in a few short sentences.

We all know that we have different levels of knowledge, and among the most intense for any of us is that knowledge we feel in our bodies. You learn how to ride a bike when you're young; you never forget how to do so again when you're older. Your body 'remembers' what to do. So it is with our Purpose. Integrating your Purpose on a physical level helps to fix the 'idea' of what your Purpose is into living, breathing reality. There are also some suggested ways of actioning it immediately. I like to engage with my Purpose in this way while I am working, and especially when I feel the need to focus and clear my mind. It never seems to wear off and has now become a natural part of my body language.

5. If your Purpose was a stance or posture, it would probably be something like . . .

Stand or create the shape you feel your Purpose is likely to be. Become aware of your posture and what it is expressing in you.

How much does it say 'Yes' to you out of 10? What would you have to do to move it up to a 9 or 10?

6. If you were to translate that stance or posture into a hand movement or gesture, you would do something like . . .

How appropriate a match is your gesture to the posture from the previous answer?

If you were going to make it more appropriate you might do something like . . .

Could you do this gesture discreetly in a way that nobody else would know what you were doing? If so, do it now.

Practise engaging with your gesture several times and see how much it reminds you of the quality of your Purpose. Change it or enhance it until it does.

The hand movement or gesture you have come up with in answer to question 6 is something you can always do to engage with your Purpose. You can do it in meetings to keep you on track, in conversations, while thinking or planning, while walking, before doing exercise, in the bath and so on. Whenever and wherever you are, you can practise engaging with it. Nobody will ever notice what you are doing, but you will know and that makes all the difference. As with all instinctive actions, simply repeating this gesture brings your Purpose back to the forefront of your mind. The more you bring your Purpose into your thoughts, feelings and actions the more you create from that point and the richer your results become.

7. If your Purpose was represented by an object it might be something like . . .

If there is a physical object that speaks very strongly to you of your Purpose you may want to have it with you or in a prominent position to act as a reminder. Sometimes these objects just come to you out of the blue when you start to focus on your Purpose.

I was in a jewellery shop one day, browsing while on a weekend away. A friend of mine suggested a highly unusual ring for me to try on. I tend not to wear much jewellery and I would never have looked at it of my own accord but I tried it on nonetheless. It fitted perfectly and felt so appropriate and clean, like King Arthur pulling Excalibur from the stone, that I bought it. I wear it to this day and it is a constant reminder to me of one aspect of my Purpose. Sometimes these things take you by surprise, so keep an eye out and see if anything comes forward.

I would stress that any object you choose is simply an object. It does not pay to be attached to it. Your Purpose is where your power lies and no object will give that to you. It can, however, be a valuable reminder and trigger in everyday life.

8. *Actioning these ideas*
Try some of these:

- Cook the meal.
- Go to the gallery or get a copy of your Purposeful picture. You could draw or paint it.
- See the film or read the relevant part of the book that reminded you of your Purpose.
- Find stories in newspapers and magazines that speak of your Purpose or search the Internet.
- Share your Purpose with others.
- Think of five other ways and action those.

Your Purpose is your essence. As a result it likes to make the most of time and opportunities and it likes to get to the point. If you imagine that on the inside you are a garden, your Purpose is a seed that has been planted deep within you. As with any living thing, feed and nourish it with love and attention and it will grow strong. The stronger it becomes, the more fulfilled and complete you will be.

ATTITUDE

There is a story about a large steamboat which broke down in Sydney harbour in the early part of the nineteenth century. The captain called out an engineer who arrived at the boat carrying a little black bag. When he went down to the engine room he began knocking on the pipes and smelling the air. Eventually he made his way to the far corner of the room, opened his bag and took out a little hammer. He tapped it three times on one part of a small pipe and put it back into his bag. 'Fire up the engines,' he called. The engines roared into life. He gave the captain his invoice for $5,000.

'Five thousand dollars,' protested the captain. 'How dare you charge me so much. All you did was tap a pipe.'

'Yes,' replied the engineer. 'If you notice I have only charged you $5 for tapping the pipe. I charged you $4,995 for knowing where to tap.'

Our Attitude is 'the place to tap' to effect a change in our behaviours and that in turn affects our experience. When we bring our Attitude in line with our Purpose we become the results that we want.

Cultivating and developing a motivating and uplifting Attitude changes our day-to-day experience of life and positively enhances all our relationships. It is a key acupuncture point of behavioural change.

Imagine for a moment that you had chosen a Purpose that is 'Climb every mountain'. The Purpose we choose is a direction and a sponsoring intention in our lives; however, some of our behaviours may be out of alignment or actually in conflict with this. You could be halfway up Kilimanjaro with three others, arguing and bickering all the way. You would still be serving your Purpose but your behaviours could actually be inhibiting your progress. Making your behaviours integral with your Purpose smooths the flow.

Of course, if we were to give our undivided attention to our Purpose and endeavour to live every moment from that point it would become behavioural; however, how many of us are that diligent with ourselves? Our behaviours are literally how we are choosing to be at any given moment. As Neale Donald Walsch says, behaviour is *be-have*-iour. In others words whatever you are *be*ing leads to your results; to what you *have*. All change and growth must become behavioural to make a difference in our lives. Many personal development systems miss this out. They are filled with fine and noble ideas but because they are not rooted in our behaviour, they die. An idea can only ever be as strong as the behaviour that backs it up. For the moment your Purpose is a strong and compelling idea about how you would like to live your life; it is your highest possibility. For that possibility to become reality we have to live and breathe it and that comes down to behaviour. If Purpose were a destination, Attitude would be the car that helps get you there.

The only guideline to what is a helpful Attitude to behave your Purpose is that it has to be beneficial to both ourselves and others; we are communal animals. The way we treat others is the way we look upon ourselves. As time goes on our lives become closer and more intertwined with others, our actions have a direct impact on them and theirs on us. We are connected and there is no getting away from that. Therefore the Attitude we will develop in this section will aim to serve the benevolent evolution or 'benevolution' of the whole. Everything else won't work. Why? Because the universe is governed by cause and effect. Therefore behaviour breeds behaviour. If our behaviour doesn't serve the general good ultimately that will impact back on us. How do we ensure a benevolent future for ourselves? By ensuring a benevolent impact on others. Remember the example of the geese, from earlier in the book? As well as flying in V formation to give themselves that legendary 71 per cent extra lift, they also adopt certain behaviours that make sure that they get where they want to go. They help each other in the following ways:

When a goose gets tired or is sick, two others drop down to rest and stay with it. Three is the minimum needed to

create a mini V to catch up with the others. Caring about each member of the community ensures that they thrive as a species. It is compassion in action.

They travel extraordinary distances in their migration paths. As they fly they 'honk' to encourage each other and to keep the pace up. Encouragement, support and positive communication is what keeps them going. It is as important as food.

Having a Purpose brings your 'inner geese' into V formation and focuses their powers in a given direction. However, this would quickly fail if it were not supported by a fundamental Attitude of care and helpfulness. This Attitude and outlook generate key behaviours. It is these behaviours that ensure success.

The next section of the book gives us a process to generate an Attitude that supports and sustains our Purpose in the world. It's what keeps us flying.

Again the process is highly creative and, in essence, will come from you. So, how do we develop an Attitude which, like the geese, helps us grow in the direction of our Purpose?

The formula is pretty simple. Before we begin to create our chosen Attitude, let's look at some basics to provide us with firm foundations on which we can build the next stage in our development. First we will look at what sponsors a fundamentally positive outlook on life. This means, how do I choose to see that the glass is half full rather than half empty? This choice in a critical mass of situations in our life affects the way we see the world, and this in turn affects our experience of it. A positive outlook equals a positive experience, generally speaking. A negative outlook inevitably equals a negative experience of life. Our choice makes the difference between the two. Each heartbeat is a beat of our internal clock. How may have you got left? Do you want them to be upbeat or downbeat?

Second, once we have set the foundations of our outlook in place, we look to cultivate an Attitude that reinforces a love of life, is motivating and uplifting, helps us achieve our aims and fundamentally says 'Yes' to us 8, 9 and 10 out of 10. We do this by looking at great examples of people who exhibit winning Attitudes, determine what speaks to us most about their way and, using an 'Attitude diamond', generate our own way. We then look at infusing this way into our behaviours and ultimately we end up with a guiding principle that we can apply constantly in all situations. This helps to grow and sustain our Attitude so that it emerges into the fabric of our character.

Outlook and Growing 'Yesness'

The following two guiding principles are, to my mind, the foundation blocks of a healthy, positive outlook on the world.

1. *What if belief and choice were the same thing?*

I'll explain. At the core of our character and Attitude is a single sponsoring choice from which all others flow. Do we look positively or negatively on the world? Do we give or do we take? Are we part of the problem or part of the solution? These questions are essentially asking the same thing: which is, do we say 'Yes' to life?

There's a true story about a man who had two sons. He spent spells in prison for theft and assault. He suffered from alcohol abuse and bouts of depression. One son grew up to be exactly the same as his father, spending time in detention centres, getting into fights and taking drugs. The other son took a different path and got a good job and raised a family.

When both sons were asked, 'How do you account for the way you turned out?' they both gave exactly the same answer: 'What do you expect with a father like mine?'

Both sons had exactly the same upbringing with exactly the same reference points and examples; however, one son saw his father as an example, while the other saw him as a warning. The difference between the two sons was a fundamental sponsoring choice: Do I choose to make the best out of life regardless of what it throws at me, yes or no? One chose 'Yes' the other 'No.'

Before we start cultivating the Attitude that supports our Purpose we have to start making the same choice. That choice, positive or negative, determines our outlook on the world.

What if we decide that today's a bad day? When we walk across town in the mood that our decision causes, what do we notice? Do we look at the headline of a newspaper advertising famine and crisis? A broken shop window? Graffiti? The dark rain-clouds? The person who walks directly in front of us nearly tripping us up? We may be convinced that it's a bad day, but are we right?

Do you believe that the world is 'bad' today, or do you choose it?

Let's look at the alternative: what if we chose today to be a good day, what would we notice? The mother playing with her child? The couple gently holding hands at the bus stop? That top you like in the window at half-price? The driver waving another car through? We might be convinced that it really is a good day. Are we right? Again, do you believe that the world is 'good' today or do you choose it?

What if belief and choice are really the same thing? After all, they are equally powerful in determining our outcomes. Would that mean we could choose the experiences we want from life? Our moods and abilities would then no longer be arbitrary. We would be able to determine our own outlook on life and that means we would master ourselves.

If we can choose our outlook on life, we can also choose our Attitude and therefore our behaviour. Since whatever I am *being* is also what I am *having*, both in terms of my results and my experience, then simply harnessing the power of choice means I can master this human vehicle. Mastering is a state of such knowledge and proficiency that one ceases to be involved in how a thing works. It's how we move from surviving the journey of life to thriving in it. In choosing our outlook on life our moods are no longer arbitrary like the weather. We literally get to choose to have a sunny day or inner blustery showers.

When you take anything, a rock, a tree or a human being and look at it on a subatomic level, we are all made up of light – of particles of energy. There was an experiment conducted in the States to find out if there is any pattern to the movement of electrons. The reasoning behind the experiment was: if we can discover the nature of the building blocks for matter, we can discover a pattern to everything solid; i.e. if I understand how a brick responds to the world then I will know how a building is likely to respond and then a town and ultimately a planet and so on.

The movements of a single electron were mapped on a screen. To find a place to start, the scientists decided they would see how many times in the seemingly random movements of the electron it moved to the top of the screen. Immediately the electron began moving upwards.

They marked down the results. Next they wanted to know how many times it moved to the left. The electron started moving to the left. Next to the right: it moved to the right, and so on. The scientists soon started to realise that wherever they chose to look affected the electron's flow. It follows then that if the little pieces of matter respond to our choices, when those little pieces make big pieces they will respond to our focused will.

Your focus steers the flow of matter. Your choices affect *your* world and *the* world.

Imagine, then, if you could choose to say 'Yes' consistently 8, 9 and 10 out of 10, to life through your actions, in your relationships and through your work? What if there were a critical mass of people making positive choices every day, all electrons flowing in positive directions. How would that affect your world and that of others?

2. *You can't action a 'not'. Complete every 'No' with a 'Yes'.*

This second guiding principle encourages us to take our positive choice and turn it immediately and simply into positive action. Positive actions breed positive results.

Whenever we tell ourselves 'not' to do something it never really works. Our minds have difficulty coping with the instruction. For example, if you were a tightrope walker on a wire, halfway between the platforms, and started telling yourself, 'Don't fall, don't fall.' Do you think that would make you more or less inclined to fall?

'Don't fall', as an instruction, is a 'not'.

Imagine you were going to walk out on stage in front of a large auditorium full of people to give a talk. The spotlight is on you. The audience is hushed, you hear your breathing through the microphone in front of you and you say to yourself, 'Don't be afraid, don't be afraid, don't be afraid.'

Does it work? Can you effectively action 'not being afraid'?

Whenever we give ourselves a negative instruction our minds simply focus on what it can picture or create. When we picture being afraid more than being confident we send our electrons in that direction and end up encouraging the outcome we would most like to avoid. We are the imaginations of ourselves in action, or 'imaginactions'. You, me and everyone else are just big walking plasma screens playing out whatever our imaginactions direct, so it's important to find ways of directing it well.

I once had a coaching client who wished to lose weight. She was unhappy with her shape and had been dieting for months to little effect. I asked her some questions to find out about her relationship to food and meals. She told me, 'I eat a lot of salad and vegetables, but what I really want is chocolate cake and biscuits.'

'So, in fact, every time you sit down to eat, you are in denial and sacrifice?'

'Well, yes, I suppose so.'

'The trouble is,' I replied, 'you can't action a "not", and your whole dietary system is based on "not eating", rather then any positive intention of becoming slim.'

We determined that what she really wanted was to look good for her cousin's wedding in six months' time. So we created a positive cycle for her: rather than saying 'no' to the chocolate cake, she changed this to say 'yes' to her positive image of herself at her cousin's wedding.

She looked great – and happy – on the big day.

We can action a 'yes' over a 'not' simply by re-formulating it in our mind: so 'not fearful' equals 'being confident'. In the example of the tightrope walker we would replace 'not falling', with the positive suggestion of 'balance' or 'moving towards the opposite platform'. As these actions are positive they enable us to act out our strongest intention and we naturally become happier and more effective.

The simplest way of looking at this idea is to take the metaphor of a battery. Electricity naturally flows from negative to positive; 'no' is negative, 'yes' is positive. To keep us in a flow of progress and to move forward with our Purpose, we must constantly move towards the posi-tive. The moment we stay in the negative zone the current stops and our energy stagnates and dies. Completing every 'no' with a 'yes' simply moves the energy forwards and we progress positively.

Is this a process of denial? No. Positive living accounts for the negative. It is a part of life. Identify and see it, yes, then move on. Notice that the negative sign '-' is half the positive sign '+', i.e., it's only halfway there. This notion is just another way of looking at the Yes Factor. Imagine that all your 'not' thoughts are in the 2, 3 or 4 zone and all your most positive ones in the 8, 9 and 10 zone. Only action 8s and above. As we do this we become naturally more effective. After a while these thoughts become second nature and we start to train ourselves to cultivate a 'Yes' outlook.

So from our earlier example:

- Our thoughts: 'don't fall' *moves to* 'balance'.

  Or this works in:

- Our words: 'the problem is . . .' *moves to* 'the answer is . . .' or 'the answer could be . . .'
- Our actions: 'managing stress' *moves to* 'creating calm'.

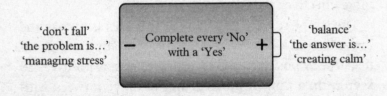

Now it's your turn. Think of three ways in which you tell yourself and others 'not' to do something. How would you formulate those thoughts and words to generate positive outcomes?

Our 8, 9 or 10 behaviours: what we think, say, feel and do are our Purpose expressed. These two guiding principles help positivity become the core and theme of that expression and positive actions lead to positive results. So . . .

What's it to be: *positive inaction*, or *positive in action*?

The choice for 'yes' gives us a foundation on which to build. Now we will devote ourselves to creating the Attitude that helps turn our Purpose into deeply fulfilling and enabling behaviours.

The Attitude Diamond

In this section we will start expressing our Purpose through Attitude.

Defining your Purpose is an inner process of articulating your deepest truth. Attitude is an external expression of that Purpose through behaviour, helping us to develop relationships with ourselves and others from our highest point of helpfulness, positivity and engagement with life. As a result our process for discovering and naming this Attitude is active.

The following is a five step recipe for cooking up your Purposeful Attitude. You will need your notebook and pencil. I suggest completing the whole Attitude section in one sitting. It usually takes about an hour.

Whereas the seven questions for the Purpose section asked you to consider and contemplate, this section invites you to dive in and take part. Please trust your experience over your thoughts; to enjoy a meal to the full, you need to taste the food, not just smell it.

Okay, when you've rolled up your sleeves and are ready for action, turn over.

1. Attitude icons

Choose three people whose Attitudes you admire and respect. These people could be alive or dead, fictional or real. They could also be people you know. It is not important that you know much about their lives or if your view of them is accurate. They do not have to be well known or to have achieved great things, only their attitude is important. How helpful, effective and inspiring are they?

The only guidelines for nominating your three Attitude icons are:

- You must respect their values.
- You must be motivated and inspired by their example.
- Their Attitude must be helpful to themselves and others.

Yes Factor your choices.

Write their names around a basic diamond shape. I developed the diamond shape because it is very hard to identify the essence of a person's Attitude, whereas you can name *facets* of that Attitude.

The basic principle is you can't see the wind, but you can see the sail and you get an idea of how the wind is behaving from the sail. In the same way, it is hard to sum up a person's Attitude in one word; however, we can label facets of that Attitude and in so doing, start to feel the essence.

E.g.:

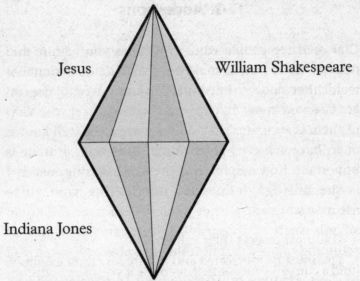

Jesus

William Shakespeare

Indiana Jones

- Have a look at your three together: If somehow you could blend their Attitudes together and come up with one of your own, how much would that say 'Yes' to you out of 10? How complete would it feel? If you are below an 8, who or what would you need to pop you into a 9?

2. Adverbs

Take each name in turn and write down seven words that describe aspects of that person's Attitude. Only choose words that can be turned into adverbs (i.e. that can end in the letters 'ly'). For example, confident > confident*ly*, inspiring > inspirational*ly*. Adverbs are *active* words, describing a quality of being. We are going to create behaviours from this point so the words you choose must be practical. In certain circumstances you may want to use a word that does not naturally convert itself to an adverb, such as 'integrity'. If you can find a way of actioning that word, put it down; for example, can you hold a conversation 'with integrity'? If you cannot, reconsider your choice of words until you find ones that are clearly active. If you're stuck, try using a thesaurus.

Write your words next to their corresponding name around the diamond as if you were labelling individual facets of their Attitude.

It is likely that several of your words will be repeated within the three lists and that some of the words will have similar meanings, which is fine.

3. Refining

Out of your list choose three words (one from each list) that stand out for you as being the keys into your diamond Attitude. If you are having trouble narrowing down your list to three, try using the same combining process as used during the tombstone process (page 45). My choices are marked with ✋.

E.g.:

Jesus	William Shakespeare	Indiana Jones
Compassion > *compassionately*	Passionate	Playful
Love > *lovingly*	Complete	Stylish
Perfect > *perfectly*	Free ✋	Boyish
Giving > *generously*	Beauty	Adventurous ✋
Noble > *nobly*	Creative	Spontaneous
Trusting > *trustingly*	Sensual	Committed
Complete ✋ > *Completely*	Natural	Sexy

Is your combination likely to be fun and enjoyable as well as effective and inspirational?

As you choose your words be aware that the ones that stand out for you do not necessarily exclude the others on the list. They are simply the ones that speak loudest to you of that person's particular Attitude.

4. In the manner of the word

This is a classic party game put to a different use. Use this section to create, practise and develop your attitude. It's designed to generate experiences, and help you choose the behaviours you find most helpful and uplifting. It's an exercise in the form of a game. You can't think it through; you have to play, and see what happens. The most truthful response is the one you have spontaneously; just have a go. It's also a great game to play with others.

• Take the three words you chose in step 3 and perform any of the following actions and/or others you think of 'in the manner of' your word. For example, if one of your words is 'adventurously' and the action is 'dance', you would have to 'dance, adventurously'. If the word is 'charismatic' what would you do if you were to dance 'charismatically'?

Below is a list of possible actions you could perform 'in the manner of' your words. Try them and others you may think of. They are a mixture of different quality of actions, from the ordinary (brushing your teeth) to the sophisticated (running a meeting) to give us experience of our words in action in a cross-section of circumstances.

• Try each of your words with a number of actions until you feel you have a good idea of what it's like to behave in that way.

You may feel more inclined to start pretending you are riding a horse or lassoing cattle if you are on your own in the middle of your living room rather than at work or in a café. In the list of actions below are many that you can practise in private. These are indicated so: *. Alternatively, you can make up your own. Give yourself a little encouragement and stretch yourself a bit.

If you would like to play this as a game with friends here's how it works. One person (player A) decides on what Attitude adverb they would like to experience. The rest of the group then makes a circle around them and asks them to perform different actions 'in the manner of the word', such as 'Brush your teeth in the manner of the word' or 'Ride a horse in the manner of the word'. The player A then has to mime that action in the manner of their Attitude word. The rest of the group tries to guess what the word is. They can have three guesses before calling out another action for player A to perform. After three actions player A tells them the word.

Whether or not the group guesses the answer correctly is not important. The guesses they put forward will almost always be reflections of other aspects of the Attitude player A is generating. For example if I am in the centre of the circle and the attitude I choose is 'encouragingly', guesses from the group may include words such as 'warmly', 'enthusiastically' and 'understandingly'. Listening to the guesses will inform me of extra dimensions of the word I have chosen.

The actions opposite are just to help get you started in your game.

Drink a cup of tea, in the manner of the word.

Brush your teeth, in the manner of the word.

Get up in the morning, in the manner of the word.

Have a telephone conversation . . .

Cook dinner . . .

Ride a horse . . .

Write a letter . . .

Jump up and down . . .

Listen . . .

Brush your hair . . .

Walk across the street . . .

Light a fire . . .

Get dressed . . .

Sing a song . . .

Lasso cattle . . .

Hold a dinner party . . .

Have a conversation . . .

Ride a dolphin . . .

* Hold a meeting . . .

* Conduct an interview . . .

Accept an Oscar . . .

Dig a trench . . .

* Listen to music . . .

* Have a bath . . .

Walk across hot coals . . .

Run . . . skip . . . jump . . .

Swim . . .

Conduct the symphony orchestra . . .

Be Tarzan . . .

Do ballet . . .

Surf a tidal wave . . .

Do the washing up . . .

Play Playstation . . .

Garden . . .

Sculpt . . .

Make clay pots . . .

Give a gift . . .

Be a cowboy . . .

Undress . . .

Speak on the telephone

Repair your car . . .

Play poker . . .

* Give a presentation . . .

Score the winning goal of a cup final . . .

Put up shelves . . .

Share your feelings . . .

Sing 'Happy Birthday' . . .

* Solve complex problems . . .

Share your Purpose . . .

>>>

Once you have tried your words individually start to merge them using more than one word at once. For example merging 'adventurously' with 'completely' and performing actions in the manner of both words simultaneously gives a very different experience to using 'adventurously' on its own. What does that feel like and how does it affect your quality of behaviour?

Eventually merge all three words to see what qualities that brings. Try them out on a variety of different tasks from the ordinary to the sophisticated. An ordinary action might be 'brushing your teeth'. A sophisticated one might be 'having a meeting' or 'entertaining'. Witness how you naturally respond and how the Attitude is helpful and empowering to you. If, for any reason, you are finding your words limiting, choose a different combination until it feels whole and complete.

Practise all three words together until you feel they have merged and you are aware of how that feels and the behaviour it encourages in you.

Try your Attitude out and honestly grade yourself with the Yes Factor on how completely you went for it. What would you do to give yourself 8, 9 or 10 out of 10?

5. Naming the Attitude

When you have your three words merged together and they are working for you, start to ask yourself what that experience reminds you of, or what you might call it if it had a name.

The name is for you. It does not have to make sense to anyone else. It describes a quality in such a way that you can connect to it time and time again.

For example:

One woman who did this exercise chose Madonna, Nelson Mandela and her mother as her three key icons of Attitude. At the end of our session I asked her to come up with a keyword or phrase to describe her Attitude and she said, 'I don't know, Rich, the only thing that springs to mind is *Red Bra*.'

'Okay,' I replied, 'could you drink that cup of tea Red Bra-ly.'

She picked up the cup and with a sassy, confident and reassured quality drank the tea. 'Red Bra-ly' made perfect sense to her. The first thing she did after the session was buy a red bra.

At the time she worked for a stiff law firm. It was a formal and cerebral atmosphere and for someone who wants to live life 'Red Bra-ly' she was finding it tough going to express that part of herself. However, for the following week she determined to make several phone calls per day 'Red Bra-ly' as well as other actions. She found that while the nature of her work did not change, her experience of doing the work was radically different. She started enjoying her phone calls and that spread to her relationships with her colleagues. Her confidence grew and her personality blossomed.

One of the Attitudes I developed for myself some years ago was *'Silver Harley'*. My combination of people brought me to generate an experience that was active, free, forward-looking and laid back at the same time. I also ride a silver Harley-Davidson-style motorbike. I discovered that riding my bike helped me actively develop these qualities. I could be engaged and active yet relaxed at the same time. Through playing 'in the manner of the word' I brought this quality into my training sessions, my physical exercise, my relationships, cooking and every-where else I could think of. Practising yoga *'Silver Harley-ly'* brought me into a very powerful engagement with the exercises while at the same time sustaining a clear, free and open state of mind. I learned that the more laid back I am, the better the bike handles in corners. This seemed to me to be a perfect metaphor for living. In generating the quality of my behaviours in this way, I am behaving my Purpose; and my Attitude enables me to connect with this in every situation, both at work and at play. The quality of my actions determines the quality of my outcomes.

My wife chose *'Olé-ly'* which spoke to her of passion, sensuality and flair for life. Another client of mine, the CEO of a business, chose *'Humanly'* which spoke to him of simplicity, kindness and timeless values. Imagine how that changes the way he deals with his colleagues and clients.

When we originally ran this exercise within my company, the collective Attitude we created was '*Sassy Surfing*', which combined everybody's individual Attitude icons and gave us an experience of dynamism, flow, harmony with the elements, fun and engagement. Within a week, everybody came into the office dressed in hip and funky ways. It also affected the way we ran meetings, laid out our offices and designed our logos and business cards. Results were better, and we had more fun.

Create a word or a term that speaks of your experience of your three words and which you would enjoy exploring for a month or more. Write your term inside your diamond, then note it daily or weekly in your diary so you can use it in work and play for at least a month

Congratulations! You have now named your Attitude.

The application of your chosen Attitude in daily behaviours is step 2 in the creation of your personal manifesto for living. There is no right or wrong. Throughout the process you have consistently asked yourself: 'What's the highest possibility I can conceive of for myself?' and chose to action that so that you can live and give your 8, 9 or 10 life as opposed to anything else. Actioning your Purpose through your behaviours says, 'This is how I choose to *become* the highest possibility I name for myself.'

Between here and the end of the Attitude section we

will look more closely at integrating and becoming the changes we would most like to bring about. In the Means section we will take these developments to a much greater scale.

Generating Behaviour: Maps and Guiding Principles

Once you have the word or phrase that sums up the Attitude you would like to explore, it's time to help turn good intentions into powerfully enabling behaviours so that they enter into the tapestry of our character.

Our Purpose is what motivates us; our behaviours are its vehicle. Through living the behaviours of our Attitude, our lives become an active reflection of our core values and we cease to create the levels of inner conflict we once held. We become deeply at peace with ourselves and our actions take on a streamlined flow. This does not happen overnight. It is a gradual, step-by-step process. The process we are about to embark on is one of cultivation, helping us grow our favoured Attitude and behaviours each and every day.

We will use a tool called the behaviour map. This is simply a way of identifying helpful and unhelpful behaviours so that we have a choice as to which ones we would like to embody. Here's how it works.

Behaviours can be defined by what we think, say, feel and do. When these are in alignment with each other, we are very powerful. When they are not, we are in conflict with ourselves.

For example:

Imagine you are a manager in a business. You may *think* that the statistics and market analysis of a particular project look positive; however you may *feel*, intuitively or emotionally, that a project will not succeed. You may *say* that there is a good chance of success, especially if others say so. What you may *do* in that situation is try to displace the responsibility for taking a risky decision by copying in others on copious e-mails, procrastination and through indecisive actions.

In relationships, we may have an argument with a loved one. We may *think* that the other is right, but *feel* hard done by and so we *say* and *do* things that are hurtful to the other as a way of getting revenge.

In both situations our four levels of behaviour are out of alignment with each other, making it almost impossible to achieve the outcomes we would most like. It is a bit like a chariot being pulled by four horses, each moving in a different direction. The chariot does not move and it suffers huge strain through the conflicting tugs. If we were to bring our behaviour into alignment we would simply honour the integrity of each one and our horses would come together, allowing us to make fast progress with little effort. In the example of the manager, we could simply voice our feeling of trepidation and ask the opinion of others. Often other people hold the same view as us but are afraid to voice it in case they are the only ones. By simply speaking out we can gauge a response and then change our actions accordingly – with integrity.

In the relationship example, if we were to admit that we suspect the other person is right but that we still feel sore, both people are likely to remain more open to one another and we are unlikely to exact the revenge that continues the chain of resentment and hurt.

In looking to align our actions we develop a sense of integrity about what we think, say, feel and do. All actions taken from this point have a far greater chance of success and have a quality of honour about them.

The behaviour map is simply a way of understanding how the four levels of behaviour align together. It helps us become conscious of how we behave in any given Attitude on a 2, 3 or 4 out of 10 and an 8, 9 or 10 out of 10. It encourages us to develop a guiding principle for the Attitude so that we can access it instantly in all situations.

For example, I recently sat with a coaching client. He was experiencing difficulties with a colleague. As he wanted to focus on his working life during the session, we were developing his ideal leadership Attitude, and used the following behaviour map to see if it would bring some clarity and a way ahead. His chosen Attitude was 'inspirationally helpful' and he wanted to know how he could become that more.

We drew our simple behaviour map, as laid out below and wrote: 'When I am inspirationally helpful . . .' at the top. We continued: 'On a 2, 3 or 4, I think things like . . .' He wrote 'Get rid of him. He doesn't respect me.' 'I say things like . . .': 'You don't now what you're talking about.' 'I feel things like . . .': 'Frustration.' 'Do things like . . .' etc. And wrote down our answers. We did the same for his 8, 9 or 10.

When I am inspirationally helpful . . .

| On a 2, 3 or 4 | | On an 8, 9 or 10 |

I think things like:
He doesn't respect me.
Get rid of him.
I can't be bothered.

I say things like:
You don't know what
  you're talking about.
Just do it!

I feel things like:
Frustrated.
Annoyed.
Separate.
Superior.

I do things like:
I ignore him.
Criticise him for other
  things.
Drink too much coffee.

I think things like:
We work really well
  together.
He's a good man.
Things are promising.

I say things like:
Well done.
You're one step ahead
  of me.
'Let's' and 'we'.

I feel things like:
Inspired.
Refreshed.
Connected.

I do things like:
 Invite him out for
  lunch.
Grow our relationship.
Take more time for
  myself.

> *My Guiding Principle:*
> *AS I GIVE, I RECEIVE*

After completing his map, we examined his 8, 9 and 10 behaviours. I asked him if there was anything he noticed about *how* he was at his most effective. He remarked that his behaviour became geared towards 'us' and 'we' in his 8, 9 or 10, as opposed to 'you' and 'I' in his 2, 3 or 4. This made him instantly more collaborative, which is another crucial key to his success as a leader. He came to a realisation, through this process, that the more he gives of his 8, 9 or 10 possibilities the more he receives.

I asked him to articulate this clearly in fewer than ten words as his guiding principle at the foot of his behaviour map, to which he wrote: 'As I give, I receive'. He determined that he would give more of himself and listen more in his leadership tasks and interactions and see how that would change things.

That afternoon he phoned me up: 'You're never going to believe this. I just got off the phone with the guy I was frustrated with. He had done a piece of work before I asked him to and I just blurted out, "Well done, you're one step ahead of me,"' (which was exactly what he had written under his 8, 9 or 10 column on the map). He laughed and felt uplifted and vibrant for the rest of the day. Now he is trying the same thing on everyone with whom he works. He is already actioning his ideal leadership Attitude in his behaviours, which is not only breeding new results but radically altering his experience of work and the people around him.

You can see how using your Attitude is a step towards putting your Purpose at the heart of everything you do. Try a behaviour map for yourself:

1. Make a copy of the behaviour map on a clean page in your notebook.

When I am . . .

On a 2, 3 or 4		On an 8, 9 or 10

I think things like . . .

I think things like . . .

I say things like . . .

I say things like . . .

I feel things like . . .

I feel things like . . .

I do things like . . .

I do things like . . .

Guiding Principle:

2. Complete the following sentence: One task I perform where I typically behave on a 2, 3 or 4 is . . . (Choose one that you have already worked on from the list on page 121, or you may want to choose an ordinary activity such as 'filing' or 'washing up' rather than a big life-changing issue for the moment. If you respond well to this try others later.)

3. What would you consider to be the most helpful Attitude you could adopt in this situation, however

unlikely? Your answer must say 'Yes' to you 8, 9 or 10 out of 10.

4. Write 'When I am . . .' plus your answer to the previous question alongside the diagram you've drawn, and then fill in the blanks.

E.g.:

I *think* things like . . .
I *say* things like . . .
I *feel* things like . . .
I *do* things like . . .

5. When you have completed the map, have a look at your 8, 9 or 10 results and see if there is anything you can learn about how you are at your best. Is there a quality or intention that goes through all aspects of your behaviour? What key learning do you derive from your 8, 9 or 10 answers? If you had to sum that up in a guiding principle, you might say something like . . .

6. Write your answer in the box. The next time you attempt the task you chose in step 2, apply your guiding principle and see it move from a 2, 3 or 4 up to an 8, 9 or 10.

7. Take your chosen Attitude (which you defined at the end of stage 5, on p.125) and apply it to the behaviour map.

Draw another template or download one from the

website: www.one-purpose.com. Simply move through the map as we have just done. If there is a strong guiding principle that occurs to you, having completed this exercise once already, write it down; otherwise complete steps 1 to 7 and form your guiding principle afterwards.

Being the Changes

Guiding principles are practical wisdom. They express the heart and essence of our character and Attitude. If my Purpose is the direction I have chosen in my life, my guiding principles are my navigation tools – my compass and my sextant. They are key generators of Purposeful behaviour. Having a variety of guiding principles to which we adhere in life is precious beyond value. They act as a constant reminder of higher wisdom and truth when times are foggy and, as any navigator will tell you, several points of reference define the way forward.

The keys to being able to use and live by a guiding principle are:

1) Having it clearly articulated in a sentence, phrase or saying.
2) Understanding it through stories and examples.
3) Choosing to apply it and see where it leads.

If you were a goose, what might your guiding principles be?

1) Align and prosper.
2) All for one.
3) Survive and thrive.

Here are some of my key guiding principles. What are yours?

1. We must become the changes we seek in the world

There is a famous story about Gandhi, who, when working in the fields one day was approached by a woman with her child. 'Gandhiji, Gandhiji,' she said, 'please could you ask my son to stop eating so many sweets.'

Gandhi looked at the boy and his mother and said, 'Come back in two weeks' time.'

Two weeks later the woman returned with her son. 'Please ask my son to stop eating so many sweets,' she repeated.

Gandhi reportedly turned to the boy and said, 'Don't eat so many sweets.'

'Is that all you are going to say?' said the mother, dismayed.

'Yes,' said Gandhi.

'Then why did you ask me to come back in two weeks' time?'

'Because two weeks ago,' he replied, 'I was eating sweets.'

This guiding principle, 'We must become the changes we seek in the world' is the essence of integrity.

2. Fire can warm you or it can burn your house down

Power is power.
Cause and effect is cause and effect.
As you sow, so shall you reap.
What goes around comes around.

There are certain fundamentals in the nature of the universe that rule our lives and that of everyone on earth. The power that we hold can work for us or against us. We have a will and we have the ability to choose. How do you use yours? To create or destroy? To hurt or to help? To give or to take?

3. *You don't have to die to go to heaven, you just have to stop going to hell*

The pain we experience from memories of things that happened to us twenty years ago is not twenty years old. It is a day old. We recreate it every day, and if we want to be free of it we have to stop creating it and start building something new.

When we were born we were infinitely creative and naturally happy. If we have lost some of this it is because we have learned behaviours and beliefs that divert us from our real selves. To get back to heaven we just have to let go of what does not work and start to experience what does.

Our Purpose is our 8, 9 or 10 choice for ourselves in this life. We also have the Yes Factor so we can continually choose to live in the 10 zone. Let go of everything that is below an 8 and you will be in heaven.

4. *Lead by serving, serve by leading*

Back in the time of the ancient Celts, Britain, known as the Island of the Mighty, was governed by regional kings with a High King who united them all. When a new High King was proclaimed the regional kings would go to him, prostrate themselves before him and place the High King's foot on the back of their necks to demonstrate the absolute nature of their devotion. Afterwards they would face the High King directly and say, 'I own you, King.' They understood implicitly that the Purpose of leadership was to be of service to the community. Despotism and power for its own sake had no credibility. The principle remains true in every walk of life where quality of leadership is important.

5. Seek first to understand

Most of the time we do not really listen, we simply wait to speak. Which means that we are not communicating, learning or growing. One-way communication is thought-traffic. True listening is feeding, learning and nourishing all rolled into one. It is the doorway to sharing and relationship. Until we start listening we are using a telephone without an earpiece.

6. Less is more

Winston Churchill said, 'I only had an hour so I wrote you a letter. If I had had longer I would have written you a postcard.'

7. A master does not create students; a master creates masters

This is a strong guiding principle to me as a facilitator. A true master acknowledges the freedom and unique collection of talents of each one of their students. Focusing on their mastery rather than their dependence helps that come into being. A true master has no need of the devotion and worship of others; that is the behaviour of dependence, not freedom. A true master would do what they do even if nobody in the world took notice, just because that is who they are and they live true to themselves. According to this guiding principle any individual or organisation who encourages greater dependence on them as opposed to increased liberation is trying to use people for their own ends.

The world needs more masters.

NOW

Start a collection of the guiding principles that you find helpful, wise and empowering. Think of them as a way of turbo-charging your Purpose statement; that way the ones you pick will be in tune with your Purpose from the start. For example: if your Purpose statement is

I serve the Purpose of enabling others to fly,

and you choose to apply Gandhi's principle of 'We must become the changes we seek', it means that you have to learn to fly first, and, as you do so, you enable others.

Choose to apply them in as many different circumstances as you can and be mindful of what the principle asks you to do. The principle will lead you and your results will follow. Remember, you cannot know at the outset exactly what actions your guiding principle will encourage in you. All you can know is that it holds a truth and a deep resonance for you. As a consequence you will surely get the results you seek.

Applying our Attitude and Guiding Principle in Everyday Life

To cultivate the Attitude supporting our Purpose practise it daily for a month, at the same time as completing the rest of this book. This way it becomes habit and enters into the fabric of our being. Choose to apply your Attitude in exactly the same way as the 'in the manner of the word' game, on three different levels of task:

1. *Ordinary*: tasks that are habitual and rudimentary require us to be conscious to a limited degree. For example, brushing teeth, getting dressed, walking to the tube, putting the kettle on.

2. *Unconscious*: Unconscious actions include breathing (unless you use your breath consciously), blinking, sitting, walking.

3. *Sophisticated*: tasks such as holding a telephone conversation, running a meeting, cooking dinner, writing a letter; all these involve multiple facets of ourselves and so are sophisticated in essence.

- Every day choose at least one ordinary, one unconscious and one sophisticated action to perform 'in the manner of' your Attitude. Keep this going for a month.

- At the end of the month, revisit the behaviour map you filled out for this Attitude and develop a guiding principle for it.
- Choose a task you habitually perform on a 2, 3 or 4 and choose to perform on an 8, 9 or 10 'in the manner of' your Attitude. The following syntax will help:

An ordinary task I currently perform on a 2, 3 or 4 is: Running this meeting. If I were to do this *'Silver Harley-ly'* I might do something like:

1) *Sit back in my chair.*
2) *Listen to what other people have to say.*
3) *Bring in more humour.*

This is a great and simple method of transforming uninspiring actions into enlivening, uplifting experiences.

A Critical Mass of Actions

Critical mass, according to how it affects our process of development, is 'the amount of actions or input necessary to create lasting change'.

There was a famous experiment where scientists observed the behaviour patterns of a particular species of monkey, simultaneously, over a number of different islands. These monkeys were not in the habit of washing their food, so to test their ability to learn and adapt, scientists rolled potatoes in sand and left them on the beach. They then watched to see how long it would take before they worked out how to eat the food.

At first the monkeys ignored the food. It was not fit for consumption. After a while, however, the young, who habitually play and experiment with their world, discovered that they could wash and eat the potatoes. The mothers, who spend most of their time with the young, soon learned this behaviour and began to follow suit.

After a while sixty to seventy monkeys had learned how to feed in this way, yet that knowledge had not spread through the tribe. The same was true when the figure crept up to eighty monkeys and even ninety: every single monkey had to make the discovery of washing their food individually. However, when the hundredth monkey had learned that it could wash and eat the potatoes, the same species of monkey on all the surrounding islands began spontaneously to clean their

143

food and eat it. The distance between the islands was significant, ruling out the possibility of contact through sight and sound. For that species with that information, the *critical mass* necessary for knowledge to enter into their collective consciousness was a hundred monkeys.

The principle of critical mass appears to be a constant in nature and is as applicable to human beings as it is to monkeys or nuclear reactions. It may explain how and why the Berlin Wall came down peacefully overnight, and why political and social movements can take on a huge momentum with so few people visibly behind them.

It seems to me that an 'internal critical mass' also exists. If we generate a certain number and consistency of thoughts, sayings, feelings and actions we create a chain reaction which shifts our consciousness. I have found that conscientiously practising an Attitude for a given period integrates the Attitude throughout our behaviours. Furthermore, within that time, we will also be setting Purposeful goals for ourselves. This will require us to fulfil a variety of tasks. Performing these 'in the manner of' our chosen Attitude brings them perfectly into alignment with our Purpose.

Thirty days seems to be the time in which practising our Attitude allows it to settle into our behaviours at an unconscious level; and using this month as a guide, we'll probably encounter most of the actions that we want to influence.

*　　*　　*

It is said that the test for a great chef is how they make an omelette. The recipe and the process are simple, it is the style in which they do it that makes all the difference. The same is true of our Purpose. Stephanie wrote:

I serve the Purpose of enabling the growth of humanity . . .

The Attitude she chose as her vehicle for this bold and clear declaration was 'skydivingly'. How she chooses to carry out her Purpose speaks something of her character. It can also determine her choices of job and lifestyle. Shortly after completing Purpose | Attitude | Means, Stephanie took some time off and went to Peru to help villagers there build wells and sanitation units. She had a direct impact on the growth and development of the people with whom she worked. Previous to this trip she had spent eight years working in an office for a large organisation. She had always felt called to do something different but did not know how to take the plunge. Her Attitude 'skydivingly' showed her a way of carrying out her actions. She took the plunge very directly and jumped into the next phase of her life feet first. Six months later she returned from Peru and decided, with her husband, to create another way of growing humanity: they now have their first beautiful child. For Stephanie, her Purpose gave her a direction, and her Attitude activated a quality of decisiveness and enthusiasm which has helped her engage with life in a new and vital way. She is a very happy woman.

Michael, who attended the same seminar as Stephanie, wrote the Purpose statement:

I serve the Purpose of being the light.

However, in stark contrast to Stephanie's way, the Attitude he devised was 'hummingly', inspired as much by Winnie the Pooh as it was by Winston Churchill. Michael's values appreciated a quieter and more gentle approach to life than the force and dynamism of Stephanie. After the seminar ended, Michael 'hummingly' moved in with his girlfriend. He 'hummingly' started his own business and 'hummingly' got married. He is a contented and loving man. His Purpose and Attitude are shining examples of the quality of love he holds and in his quiet and gentle way he generates and shines his light. Everybody has their own way and there is room for us all. Some people are rushing rivers and some babbling brooks. The Attitude we choose affects the way we travel. Michael opted for the babbling brook and it serves his Purpose admirably.

Hal is a strong and determined man. He is one of those people whom you imagine was a great warrior in a former life. His Purpose statement,

I serve the Purpose of being truth,

came as no surprise. Given his natural tendency to plough through obstacles and hold firmly to his principles he could easily have chosen Attitudes like 'fearlessly' or 'uncompromisingly'. However, when it came to determining his way I asked Hal what would combine a sense of strength and effectiveness with fun and playfulness. The Attitude he chose then was 'dolphinly'. This serves as a constant reminder to him not to take life too seriously and that the more he explores and creates in his life, the more effective he is. It was as if a weight had lifted off his shoulders. Somehow, his belief system was 'strength leads to progress', yet he could see through the example of dolphins *and* through the way employing that Attitude affected his own behaviour and action that there were other ways that were equally effective and more fun. He realised that the life he is living is the only one he has got. He could easily spend another fifteen years wrapped up with his former Attitude, but that would not take him where he wanted to be. Cultivating the Attitude 'dolphinly' had gently and directly shown him another way of life. He laughs more now.

MEANS

When baby sea turtles hatch, they dig their way through the sand and try to find the sea 100 metres or so away, instinctively moving towards the greatest light source. In a natural surrounding, that is the horizon. If they survive, the only time they will come back to the beach is when the females lay their eggs. This is approximately thirty years from the time that they hatch. They may have swum all around the world throughout their life, but they always come back to the exact same beach where they were born to lay their eggs. How do they find their way? There is a tiny crystal in their brains. When they make their first journey from the egg to the ocean, this crystal is magnetically charged with the exact longitude and latitude of the place, making it easy for them always to find their way home.

Imagine for a moment that our Purpose is a diamond inside us. When we name it in truth, the diamond is fused with our intuition in much the same way as the turtles'. We have our own built-in radar to seek out everything and everyone that help us live our Purpose to the full. The Means part of the programme is about harnessing the power of this radar, this focused and programmed intuition. We will use it to set goals which serve to create our lives as a Purpose-driven work of art, day in, day out. We will also use it to fulfil those goals, like a satellite navigation unit telling us where we are and how far there is to go.

The result is that we enter into a great flow of providence and synchronicity. We ally with others whose Purposes coincide with our own, we develop a deeper trust in the world and we accomplish our goals with an uncanny ease and enjoyment. Opportunities fall into our lap and it feels like a constantly evolving miracle. Our energy becomes focused with a laser-like concentration and so we hold a much stronger attraction for those events and people who have a similar calling. As we set our goals, our Purpose unfolds before our eyes like the yellow brick road.

As with geese, our Purpose brings our whole being into V formation – all of ourselves working for the whole. Our Attitude affects how we behave and fly, sometimes together with others. Means is our practical agenda, helping us determine our goals and stop-off points along the way, and how to navigate and stay on target.

Purpose is BIG. There's no getting around that. The course you have embarked on, if you follow it through, will change your life in ways that say 'Yes' to you 8, 9 or 10 out of 10. Visions, dreams and Purposes seem huge at first but however big they may appear, they always boil down to doing things day by day, moment by moment.

John Travolta was once asked a question about acting: 'How do you keep the whole journey of a character in your mind when performing a scene?' He replied, 'I don't. I concentrate on the journey of the individual scene, then the overall journey takes care of itself.' The Purpose | Attitude | Means process is designed to help choose a motivating direction for yourself and then give yourself to it scene by scene.

At this stage in the process people often ask, 'If my Purpose is very different to how I have been running my life does this mean that I have to change my life completely?' If we truly live our Purpose will we leave our jobs, our spouses and embark on a completely different life, wandering off into the sunset with a pack on our backs? No, you don't have to do that. The relationship or job you have in some way represents who you are at the moment. One participant who undertook this process arrived at the Purpose statement:

I serve the Purpose of growing truth.

This spoke to him on a core level; however he was in a relationship where he and his partner were avoiding issues and playing 'relationship games'. He had now discovered what was most important to him and there-fore if he was to live his 8, 9 and 10 life he would have to start to get to grips with the problems in his relationship; and the way he had chosen was truth. So, he and his partner started to sit down and do the talking they had always wanted to do but had always avoided. Gradually they began to set themselves and each other free. They are both happier and more contented with life now and say that they have found their 'true' relationship.

Nothing is fixed. Proust said, 'The real voyage of discovery consists not in seeking new landscapes, but in having new eyes.' Affecting the way we look at key areas of our life affects our experience of them. Meaning and Purpose do not inherently exist in our relationships or jobs, we put them there. Now that you know what is meaningful to you, you have the opportunity of growing those seeds where you are. This does not have to mean fast radical change. Revolution, personally and collectively, can leave scars. It is often too brusque and aggressive. I prefer to look at evolution instead. I find that there is a natural harmony in changes that evolve. It is the natural path. It reminds me of when I was watering my garden recently.

I had the hosepipe in my hand and, behaving as I do, like a boy, I put my thumb over the end of the pipe and was spraying as far away from me as I could. The reasoning in my mind was if I can spray over a greater distance, I can water the garden faster and more efficiently. Then a little guiding voice inside me suggested, 'Water round your feet.'

No, I thought, spraying is much more fun.

'Water round your feet,' it quietly insisted.

I gave in to the softness of the voice, more intrigued by what it might show me than by spraying. I started walking around the garden watering in a small radius around my feet. Very soon I had finished. It was much faster and more efficient than the other method and I felt peaceful and appropriate. Since then, I have started to see that 'watering round my feet' is a wonderful guiding principle. It invites me to take one task at a time, to progress gently and stops me putting pressure on myself to 'achieve, achieve, achieve!'

I suggest 'watering round your feet' for the time being, putting your Purpose into action in the places you go, with the people you meet and the tasks you have before you. When it comes to setting our goals in the section ahead, you may decide to make a few changes. These, however, are unlikely to be radical changes, more like the opening of new golden doorways.

Now we have to discover how to put all we have learned into practice. It's a very simple thing really. We will look at using your Purpose as a tool for setting goals in every area of your life. Then, as you follow the actions that lead to your goals 'in the manner of' your Attitude, you will be living your Purpose. Goals are your intentions, crystallised.

We will look at using your intuition as a tool to help you achieve your goals. In *The Wizard of Oz*, Dorothy learns how to make her way home by using her ruby slippers. Your intuition is like Dorothy's slippers. It will always take you where you want to go, you just have to remember to use it. We are going to treat your intuition as if it were a tool, plain and simple, a navigation device for getting you Purposeful results. Your intuition will get you there faster and it will be more of an adventure. Our intuition is both sextant and satellite navigation in one; it will always help us find the shortest distance between two points, but it does not sit well with the logical mind which likes to do things in a linear fashion. There is a new mode of transport currently being developed. The earth spins faster than we can fly, so a new hybrid of a spacecraft and an aeroplane is being designed. The plane takes off, flies to the upper reaches of the atmosphere and descends immediately. The earth has been spinning all the while. In this way we could fly from London to Australia in about an hour. The logical brain thinks it would take a standard twenty-six hours for the flight. The intuition goes the atmospheric route.

Our intuition simply finds the quickest, easiest route for us. We find out why this is so later, which requires us to pay attention and to be present to the world around us. The by-product of this quality of presence and attention is that we stop projecting how things 'ought to be' on to the canvas of the future. The mind is limited to its experience of the past and is unreliable as a source of knowledge. We have to live in the present for which the intuition is permanent radar. It will seek out opportunities for any endeavour we choose for ourselves, good or ill.

When we began this process, we aligned our intuition with our Purpose and fused them together. All we have to do is learn how to use the tool and it will always take us where we wish to go; an intuition attuned to our Purpose is like having a periscope into Provide-nce.

The logical paths to goal-setting require hard work and dedication from you. The intuitive path asks you to do two things; to trust and to listen. The only person you have to trust is yourself. Most people use their minds a lot in everyday life. They plot and plan their lives and believe that if they just cover all the angles everything will work out fine. They put in a lot of work and effort and then discover that plans never seem to go according to plan.

Now that you have your Purpose and can be-have it through your supporting Attitude, all your inner geese are aligned. You are a much more powerful person now than you were before we started. Your attention is much more focused so you have a greater ability to attract events and circumstances to yourself. This means that your clarity of intention can do a lot of the work you used to do through sweat and toil. You are simply more attractive to synchronicity.

Have you ever had the experience of wanting something and then suddenly out of the blue there are all sorts of coincidences that happen and the thing just slots into place? That 'coincidence' is 'coincide-nce'. It is literally when events coincide around a focal point. When you hold a strong intention that focal point is you. Put together, all of that is synchronicity. Because you are more attractive to synchronicity it is much easier for you to get what you want by learning how it works as a tool than it is to do things the old way. You will still have to perform actions but they will become easier and the actions you need to perform will not always be obvious to you. That is why you have to trust. When you let your intuition guide you, you have to trust it and follow where it leads.

You also have to listen, *really* listen. Your intuition has a voice that speaks inside you but it also has many other voices. It can show you things, take you to places, guide your attention to newspaper headlines, to the words in a song playing through the open window of a passing car. It can speak to you through the adverts on the bus and even through silence. Listening means listening with your eyes, your mind and your heart. That's really where the adventure starts.

How to get the most out of this section

For this section, alongside your trust and listening muscles, you'll also need your notebook and your pencil once more.

Remember, the answers you give may not make sense to you at first but tackle the questions anyway. Answering them will bring your subconscious into play and as your *whole* mind starts to come to work for you, you will see that your answers are giving you what you need.

Here are a few suggestions to help you 'get into the zone'.

1. Play the piece of music that helped you free your mind before answering the seven Purpose questions. You may also wish to play a piece of music that speaks to you of your Purpose.

2. Trigger your Purpose using the stance or hand gesture you developed in the earlier sections.

3. Allow yourself not to know what goals your Purpose may encourage in you. Your goals, and the Purposeful way of achieving them, may be different from how you assume them to be. *Follow your instincts*.

4. Allow Purpose to guide you. Let your intuition work for you by allowing it to speak.

5. Be resolutely focused on what says 'Yes' to you most on a core level.

6. Answer the *whole* of the next section in the manner of your Attitude.

Honeycomb Lives:
Setting Purpose-Driven Goals

There was a study carried out in the US where they tried to discover what made the most successful people, in their individual fields, all over the planet, successful. They considered every field of human endeavour, including sports, the arts, science, politics, business, and so on. The top 2 per cent were shown to have only one factor in common: they all, at some stage, wrote their goals down on paper. Writing them down clarified their goals and helped them to focus on exactly what it was they looked to achieve in life.

So let's start to write down some of the goals that express our Purpose.

There are twelve clear steps to setting and achieving Purpose-driven goals. They are clearly laid out below. Simply follow the process through stage by stage, listening to and trusting what comes to you through your intuition. Although much of what follows is based on our subconscious, there is a very simple unseen structure which comes from the three basic rules of navigation. This whole process adheres to these. They are:

1) Where are you now?
2) Where do you want to go?
3) How do you plot a path between the two?

1. *Draw a hexagon in the middle of a clean page with the extra lines as illustrated. Write your Purpose statement in the middle*

2. *Write a list of six major areas of your life*

Facilitation tip

Six is a good manageable number. If there are more that you would like to include in your list write them down and see if they can be brought together (you can use the same method as for tombstone). Be sure to bring in a combination that allows for your enjoyment of life, health and development as well as material success.
E.g.:

- Relationship
- Family
- Career
- Health
- Personal development
            +   } Spirituality
- Spiritual development
- Fun

Other common categories are: finance, social, travel and other personal ambitions.

3. *Put down the names of the areas that you feel most accurately reflect the major areas in your life; it's important that you look at what really matters here*

It is a good idea to limit these categories to one-word titles; this will help you to set clear goals.

Here's my example to give you an idea.

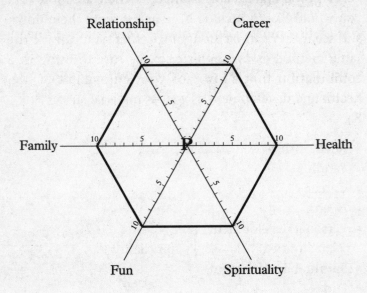

4. *Have a look at your hexagon. How complete does it feel to you out of 10 as a representation of the key areas of your life?*

If it is below a 9 out of 10, what would you have to do to move it up?

You will notice on the diagram that each of the lines

leading from the centre of the hexagon to its edge is numbered from 1 to 10. Counting the outside edge as the 10 and the centre as zero and looking at one area of your life at time, answer the following:

5. *If you were to know how much you were living your Purpose out of 10 in this area, you'd probably say . . . out of 10?*

- Mark that number down on the corresponding line.
- Move through each area asking the same question.
- When you have finished, join the dots.

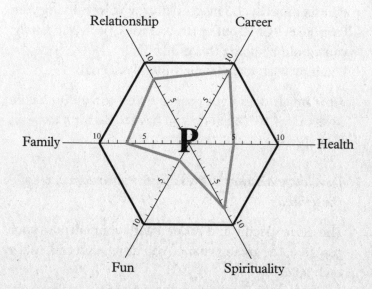

Balance is a key to harmonious living and the hexagon is a naturally balanced shape. Looking at your diagram it will become clear which places will give the clearest results if you give them your attention. These are good places to start setting goals.

6. *Set your goals*

Choose an area of your hexagon, and using your intuition complete the following.

- If my Purpose were to choose a goal for me in this area of my life it would probably say . . .

  Or

- If in six months *(1/3 months)* time, you were living your Purpose 8, 9 or 10 out of 10 . . . at *work / with your family*, you would be doing things like . . .
  You may wish to use your answer as a goal.

  How much does your goal say 'Yes' to you on a core level out of 10? What do you have to do for it to be an 8 or above?

7. *Develop goals that express your Purpose in each of these areas*

The more specific and infused with your Purpose your goals are, the greater chance you have of success. Make each goal:

Realistic: *Does your intuition think that your goal is realistic? Do you believe it?*

Achievable: *Are you setting yourself a goal that is achievable or are you trying to pile too much on yourself? Aim for balance.*

Specific: *Be clear about your goal. Generalised goals such as 'Get better at . . .' lead to generalised results. The more specific you can be the clearer your results. Tie it to time, if possible; what is the date and time by when you will have completed your goal? e.g. by Monday 17th, 5 p.m. I will have . . .*

Enhancing: *Does this move you beyond your present circumstances?*

8. *Vision the perfect picture*

Imagine that your goal has been completed perfectly. How does that area of your life look. What is going on? Describe the perfect completion of your goal. Make your picture full and vibrant. Enjoy its perfection. See as much detail as you can; if you could smell or sense or taste or listen to the quality of that moment what would be there? What would you have to do to move that image to a 10 out of 10? Include your answer to this question in your overall answer.

The subconscious mind loves metaphors and stories so the following is simply a way of engaging it more deeply as an ally in achieving your Purposeful goals: *What's it a bit like?*

Tasting it . . . running it through my mind . . . feeling it . . . it's a bit like . . .

Looking at the *quality* of your 10 out of 10 image, what does it remind you of? If it were a scene or a picture what would it be? This question is aimed at helping you engage your subconscious, so that it is truly absorbed by your whole being.

For example, when I ran my perfect vision of my relationship goal through this process the image that came to me was:

My 10 out of 10 relationship, at this time, is a bit like . . . two blue whales swimming together on the high seas, finding the sacred nourishing place to have their baby,nuzzling each other as they move, massaging and caressing each other with their sounds. In my subconscious this was an image of intimacy and tranquillity. Whatever analogies your mind comes up with, see what qualities it is suggesting to you.

This vision is a tactile, tangible one, enabling me to take my relationship to a new level of intimacy.

9. *If there were two stages before that they would be . . . ?*

The process helps you to get to that vision. We have begun with the highest possibility we can conceive of, and now we work backwards.

Getting to the quality of the 10 out of 10 vision there are two clear stages of development. If you knew what they were, you would say something like . . .

You may have unexpected answers occur with this question. That's okay. Trust them and put them down. We are working with metaphor and intuitive intelligence, which are not logical processes. They work like magic so if your answer doesn't appear to make sense yet, that's great. Go with it. The idea is to set your subconscious mind working freely on the question, and thereby engage its help and power later on.

The stages are written in reverse order so that we always complete with our perfect scenario. Drawing them in this way helps to reinforce that view.

For example, if your goal is 'buying a house', and you have created a vision of yourself walking around your new garden on a summer's evening, the preceding stages might be something like this:

>>> ***Stage 3:*** *Looking out from the porch at the stillness of your new garden.*

>> ***Stage 2:*** *Shaking hands with the owner, who hands you the keys as you complete the deal.*

> ***Stage 1:*** *Finding a house that says 'Yes' to me 8, 9 or 10 out of 10.*

Greg's Purpose statement was:

I serve the Purpose of constant evolution.

When he came to set his family goal he chose one around spending regular quality time with his wife and children, engaging in activities that drew him and them together, whereas previously he had pursued his own interests apart from them. His three stages were:

3. The Club: *Having a drink in the bar or a clubhouse, meeting new people after having played his sport, together with his children. Standing with others in a group, enjoying his wife's laughter.*

2. The Car: *Driving home with the kids playing in the back of the car, discussing with them and his wife the activities they would enjoy in the location to which they had just moved as a result of a new job.*

1. The Class: *Attending his first martial arts class with his son, learning and growing in a new field together.*

Sometimes, however, the stages towards your goal will be unexpected and may not even seem to make sense. For example, when I set my relationship goal around intimacy and tranquillity the two stages that preceded the final one were: *Finishing the book* and *Relaxed assurance.*

I could not see how either of those two stages were related to my relationship with my wife. However, working with the subconscious is an interesting experience and shortly after writing my goal and stages down I found that I started to wear different clothes to before. I engaged with my yoga and other physical practices in a new way and began feeling different and more complete in my body. I discovered a 'relaxed assurance' on a deeper and more constant basis, and my life started to feel more cleanly appropriate.

As I have been experiencing these changes, I have also been coming to the end of finishing this book, which, in an obvious and curious way, feels like closing a chapter of my life and opening the next. This is now showing itself clearly in my relationship with my wife. We have become closer, more unified and freer with each other. Our affection for each other is deeper and our respect for each other more pronounced.

When I set this goal, I had no idea that my own sense of self-assurance and the writing of the book would impact on other parts of my life so directly. I simply set the goal with and through my Purpose and adhered to the answer. The rest has been a process of discovery, as I have witnessed the unfolding of my intuition and subconscious in my life.

Because the process works with the intuition, your subconscious mind will start to move you into ways of completing your goals. How and why this works will not be obvious at the outset. It is often only when looking back at a later date that you discover how the process has unfolded; but that's the adventure.

If you're still struggling with this process, here's another way of thinking about it.

When the great Spanish architect Antonio Gaudi designed the famous Sagrada Familia Cathedral in Barcelona, he carried out an experiment. He suspended lines from a metre-high platform and tied them together at the bottom so they made an elongated cup shape. He then hung small weights from each part of every line. The result was he started to see the shape and structure of gravity. He then put a mirror on the ground underneath his experiment and looked in. What he saw was the mirror image of the shape of gravity and that became his core design for the cathedral. By taking the perfect inverse to gravity and building that – by working backwards, from his ultimate result – he created a building with an inherent natural harmony in the design.

We are adopting the same principle in the way we determine the path to our goal. Working backwards in this way helps us to bring the same natural harmony to bear.

10. *Draw icons*

Look at what you've written in stage 9, and alongside the words draw a little icon or image inside a circle which speaks of the quality of each stage. Forming anything new, including creating your Purpose goals, is a creative process. The more you engage your creative mind at the outset the easier it is for your goals to come to fruition.

Using our example of buying a house the three icons could be:

Stage 3: *Looking out from the porch.*

Stage 2: *Shaking hands with the owner.*

Stage 1: *Finding a property.*

As you can see by my sketches here, you do not have to be a great artist to draw something that speaks to you. Drawing your icons is a very valuable part of the process and helps your goals come to fruition. It's all part of making your life a work of art.

Make your personal diary your 'book of life'

If you don't already use one, my suggestion is to keep a diary to help you plan and implement your Purposeful goals, from here on in. As you complete your goals and further your Purpose, your diary will begin to become your real 'book of life'.

Once you have completed the above sections, you will have set your goals very clearly. All your energies are aligned and your Purpose will start to manifest itself. The more you put yourself into the process, the clearer your results are likely to be. Providence, the fusing of synchronicity and your subconscious, has just become your ally, so give it room to manoeuvre. As you develop these tasks below, you'll be given signals; put them in your diary and make each day count.

Now that you have clearly set your goal, there are three things to do:

1. *Listen to the gentle tugs of your intuition*

You may be drawn to talking to certain people, going to particular places or eating certain foods. *Pay attention*. Not everything you feel drawn to do will be for the reasons you think. For example, you may wish to eat in a certain restaurant. Nothing may happen there; however, you may hear a snatch of a passing conversation while leaving which will serve the fulfilment of your goal and therefore your Purpose. You may end up parking next to a shop window which advertises a product or service that may also help you.

After attending this course one man had a phone call from his brother out of the blue. They had not spoken for years. Through the conversation his brother offered him the finance he needed to move towns and get the job he wanted. At the time he attended the course he was long-term unemployed. Within two weeks Provide-nce had shown him a way.

There are a thousand ways your Purpose will reveal

itself. Allow yourself to be guided. Turn it into a game, or your own Indiana Jones adventure. Follow the clues and watch the constantly evolving miracle unfold.

2. *Do what needs to be done*

Within this process of listening to the movements of synchronicity there will be some tasks you need to perform. These will start to become obvious to you, day by day. Some you will be drawn to and others will become a persistent tug at the back of your mind as if someone is knocking on the door. As you become aware of these tasks, put them in your diary, and make each day count. Fulfil every task that comes your way in the manner of your chosen Attitude and complete them. You can always check how complete you are by using the Yes Factor:

- how complete am I on a scale of 1-10?
- To pop myself into a 9 or 10 I would have to do something like . . .

This will ensure that you are constantly engaging with your Purpose and living according to your values. You will almost certainly enjoy it. Use your common sense and watch it come to fruition naturally.

3. *Ask Purpose*

The simplest and most effective way of engaging with your Purpose on a day-to-day basis is simply to ask it, as if it were another person, to guide you. It will always steer you in the direction of your greatest meaning. Its answer may come as a feeling, a word or a picture. You may be drawn to look in a particular direction, or there may be a quality of peace and understanding present. However it talks to you is your way. Everybody's Purpose is unique. There is so much information in life, and so many possible ways of doing things. Asking Purpose to choose a path for us is engaging specifically with the energy of meaning and effectiveness. You may not understand how it works, but try it anyway and see what happens. You are simply asking that Purpose – your best little bit – runs your life.

> *Complete steps 1-10 for each area of your life or as many as you wish to work on*
Set yourself the amount of goals or challenges that feel appropriate to you now. If you set too many you may unbalance yourself and it will seem burdensome. Too few and the changes are slower.

My suggestion is to set three goals at a time.

> *Revisit your goals every 2-3 months*
- Draw a new hexagon, adjoining your previous one and repeat steps 1-3.
- Compare your 1-10 rating with the previous time.
- Has your vision of a 9 or 10 changed or grown?
- What have you learned in that time?

- How did your goal-path reveal itself?
- Set yourself new goals.

> ### *Plan a reward for every goal that you set yourself*

Most people don't spend a lot of time rewarding or recognising themselves or others. Of course it helps us enormously and as a strategy for success it's common sense, but is it common practice?

Reward and acknowledgement is a very important part of any goal-setting process and is essential for a balanced life. Purpose without fun becomes duty and that is more akin to sacrifice. Life is for living; reward and acknowledgement are our tools for celebrating that.

You can choose to reward yourself weekly, monthly, at the end of goals or at milestones along the way there. Regular reward is a good, nourishing thing. Choose what most suits you.

I suggest the following formats to set juicy rewards:

1. *Choose the goal for which you will set yourself the reward.*

2. *Name your reward.*

Any of the following formats will help you set your-self a juicy reward:
- If my Purpose were to set a reward for me, it would probably say something like . . .

- If there was one thing I could do to reward myself it would be . . .
- The reward my Purpose suggests is . . .

3. *Write your reward on the same page as its corresponding goal.*

4. *Sign and date it to reinforce it as a commitment you make to yourself.*

5. *Create a 'reward icon' in the same way as your 'goal icon'.*

6. *Put your reward in your diary.*

7. *Be sure to keep it. A reward kept = Acknowledge-Meant.*

Allow for the possibility that your Purpose may want to reward you differently when the time comes. For example, if you have promised yourself a great meal at your favourite restaurant but when it comes to that evening your partner ends up cooking you a wonderful meal and you snuggle up afterwards and watch a video, that's probably exactly what the doctor ordered. Allow your instincts to guide you.

Remember
- Carry out your goals in the manner of your Attitude, ensuring that the actions you take are motivating, inspiring and uplifting.

- You reap what you sow. Sow Purposeful seeds for a happiness harvest.

You have written your goals in your handwriting and heartwriting.
You have fused them with your intuition.
Now, let Purpose lead the way . . .

If in doubt:

Ask Purpose. Ask Purpose. Ask Purpose. Ask Purpose.
Ask Purpose. Ask Purpose. Ask Purpose. Ask Purpose.
Ask Purpose. Ask Purpose. Ask Purpose. Ask Purpose.

Ask Purpose

Ask Purpose. Ask Purpose. Ask Purpose. Ask Purpose.
Ask Purpose. Ask Purpose. Ask Purpose. Ask Purpose.
Ask Purpose. Ask Purpose. Ask Purpose. Ask Purpose.

THE PURPOSE TOOLKIT

The geese manage to navigate, stay on course, and find their way through the rough spots, achieving their endless summer; how can we do the same, living on Purpose?

As with most things in life, there are easier and harder ways of getting the results we choose. Purpose is no different. The following tools are out 'in-flight enablers' to make the journey smoother. They work with your creativity and intuition and will further help you behave more in line with the character of your Purpose. Use them as and when you feel like – this isn't a programme to follow, simply ways to help you adjust your path and keep you on a Purposeful course.

The Yes Factor

We have already used the Yes Factor extensively throughout the process so it is likely to be pretty intuitive for you by now. I use it for everything. It is a direct and simple tool for engaging with our creative/intuitive intelligence. You can use it in any number of different ways.

Ask yourself regularly:

- How much does this say 'Yes' to me out of 10?
- How much does this express my Purpose out of 10?
- How complete does this feel out of 10?
- How clear is that out of 10?

The Yes Factor is a fantastic tool at work. In meetings it helps to find out how much people are in agreement. Simply ask how much a thing says 'Yes' to everyone out of 10. When some people are below an 8, help them pop up the scale. Or when writing reports, it is always useful to ask oneself, 'How complete does this feel out of 10?' Your answer will tell you how much more work there is to do.

In relationships using the Yes Factor together with your partner can help to overcome misunderstandings and conflicts.

Choose only to action 8s and above. That way if something is a 7 for us, we simply have to ask the question: What would make this an 8, 9 or 10? And we have a simple technology for moving ourselves into the 10 zone.

In this way, we set our best intention to serve our highest choice and let our intuition fill the gap; in other words, living our Purpose.

Clarity

Speaking with clarity expresses yourself Purpose-fully

Clarity breeds confidence and is a huge enabler. Clarity of thought means clarity of communication and fulfilling most of our goals is likely to include communication in some form. This could be communication with others or with oneself; whatever the circumstances, if it is 9 or 10 out of 10 clear, it has a much better chance of succeeding. Clarity of thought, word, intention and deed is another element to living a streamlined life. It saves a lot of time and energy. Clarity is the language of Purpose. The more you can hone and develop it the easier it is for your Purpose to sing through your life.

Getting to the essence and simplicity are our foundation blocks. Here are some tools

Less is More

- Reduce everything down to its essence first. You can always elaborate later. Knowing the essence of something helps you to align it with your Purpose.
- Use fewer than ten words.

In several of the Purpose questions you were asked to write your answers in fewer than ten or fifteen words. This helps get to clarity fast. We become more creative with tighter boundaries and clearer with less time and space to get complicated. Whatever you have to say, at work, to your partner, to your children, in a letter, a report, to your bank, what would you say if you only had ten words? How about five? This will help you reduce what you want to say to what you really mean. Your actions become clear and meaningful and therefore Purpose-full.

(If you like this approach, and you find it clarifies your thoughts for you, here's a beautiful exercise you can do with sketching that extends the discipline of *less is more*. Two people face each other with sketchpads. They each draw the other using seven pencil strokes. Then using five, then three and finally one pencil stroke. The evolution to clarity is obvious through the sketches and the ones composed of fewer lines are almost always more beautiful, poetic and suggestive.)

Write your goals in five words or fewer

If you are trying to explain something complicated to someone, try kicking off with 'Basically, what I mean is . . .'

If you had thirty seconds to explain yourself you would say . . .

Creative Intuition

Anything is possible through your creative mind. Creativity and intuition 'know'. The logical mind then starts to understand. To live our Purpose means being driven by the creative/intuitive mind first and to understand it in a linear fashion second. Honing your creativity will help you solve problems and find new ways to achieve the goals you set yourself earlier. If used well it is a magic wand.

Einstein said, 'None of my great discoveries ever came through the process of rational thinking.' His imagination furnished him with theories and principles and his logical mind put them into scientific principles later. This is why artists such as Kandinsky were able to map accurately the neural pathways of the brain through their paintings years before they were visible under a microscope.

Recently while halfway up a rock-face I was confronted by an overhanging piece of rock which presented a great challenge to both my ability and strength. I tried everything I knew: face-on, side-on, backwards, forwards, using my teeth (almost!). I ended up huffing and puffing and making no progress. I was not going to get to the top of the route and was ready to give up and be lowered down when a thought occurred to me: I have tried everything I know. How about trying something I don't know. But how could I access something I don't know?

I asked myself a question: If I were a fantastic climber I would probably do something like . . . and an idea formed in my mind of a move I had not yet tried. I tried it. It worked like a dream and before I had time to flash a beaming smile at my partner, I was at the top of the route. Since then I have tried a number of different questions and have had surprising and hugely successful answers.

On another climbing route I tried the first question but did not have a clear answer so I tried another: If I knew how to scale this route I would probably do something like . . . The answer came through: 'dance'. Not quite knowing how I could dance and climb at the same time I decided to climb 'in the manner of the word'. I approached as the dancer in my imagination might and again moved through the difficulty with grace and ease. I am learning that there is always a way through any problem and that our creative minds have the keys. Our job is to find out how to tap its infinite power – and to listen.

Throughout this book questions have been posed in a way that bypasses the logical mind, asking your sub-conscious to furnish you with answers effortlessly. They tend to follow a similar format. I call these '. . .' formats since they are always open-ended and invite possibility.* They are one of the fastest and most effective routes of

* Chuck Spezzano www.psychologyofvision.com is the master of this type of questioning.

engaging the creative/intuitive mind. I recommend using them. Here's how they work:

Start with an 'if' which engages the creative mind:

- If you were to know . . .
- If there was a way . . .
- If you had three words to describe . . .

Complete the sentences with phrases like

- you might do something like . . .
- you'd probably say something like . . .
- you might feel . . .

The questions are always open-ended and asked in a way that invites possibility, and we can apply them internally or externally; the climbing examples I gave earlier illustrate some of the internal applications.

'. . .' formats are also an excellent way of gently helping others develop ideas and get to clarity. There is literally no limit to the uses of this format. You could even ask yourself, if I were to know what the best question to ask now is, I might say something like . . . or even, if I knew how to do . . . I would probably do something like . . . All we then have to do is act on the answer that surfaces.

The creative mind can sometimes behave a bit like a monkey. It likes variation and wants to experiment in all sorts of different ways. Try to expand your expectations. It is there to help you go beyond them. 'If you always do what you've always done, you'll always know what you've always known' – and where's the fun in that?

Not every question gets us exactly what we want all the time. Sometimes we have to try some variations and sense the way through. The answers that come can take many and all forms. Sometimes they appear as a question. Sometimes as a challenge. Occasionally I find I am reminded of someone or something or a line from a song might start playing in the back of my mind. I have discovered that these are all clues, which, when followed, lead to insight, learning and growth. They are also highly entertaining.

See what an idea can bring you before rejecting it.

If you're stuck, recall your Purpose-ful figures from the beginning of the process, and think about what they'd do in your shoes.

Choose to apply '. . .' formats in your internal thinking, to help you solve problems and in your day-to-day language with other people.

If you are a facilitator, run groups, have a family, or would like to help others find solutions and clarity quickly, I suggest becoming fluent with this technique.

Simplicity

If you can say something simply you probably understand it,
if you can't, you probably don't.

Say what you mean and mean what you say. Your Purpose is the most truthful part of yourself. It cannot live through your actions unless they are simple, clear and honest. If there is a filter between what you mean and what you say your energy is dissipated and your results are affected. It's like running through water.

Evolution is about refinement and refinement leads to greater levels of simplicity. Ultimately in evolving what we do we are looking to get greater results with less effort. This does not happen through becoming more complicated. Simplicity is progress.

As we evolve and our Purpose becomes more present in our life, our habits and outlook become simpler. We tend to see things with greater clarity, take pleasure from places we overlooked before and imbue each moment with its due weight and attention. The world becomes stiller and calmer and we are able to see things as they are more than as we are.

For me, simplicity has a cleanliness about it, a purity. Expressions like 'out of the mouths of babes' talk of a simplicity, an innocence and an open curiosity which asks questions out of pure intent. The simplicity which grows out of Purpose is of the same nature.

Whenever you have something to explain or a message to get across, ask yourself, 'How would I say this to a six-year-old?'

Michelangelo said, 'Inside every block of marble is the perfect statue; my job is to take away what is not that.' If you were going to apply that guiding principle in your daily life, you might do things like . . .

Collaboration

It takes two to tell the truth
Chinese Proverb

Whatever Purpose we choose for ourselves we need others for it to live. No endeavour is truly independent. Every great mission, journey and achievement in the history of humanity has involved many people. Your Purpose is exactly the same. If we can collaborate effectively it will make the realisation of our Purpose that much smoother and more enjoyable.

Great collaboration is born out of a fundamental respect for others' views and abilities. Nobody has a monopoly on truth. Research has recently revealed that astronomers are the most successful collaborators of any group of people in the world. This is because wherever they are on the planet, however big their telescope or research budget is, they can only ever see the piece of the sky above them. If they want to get a complete picture the only choice they have is to collaborate with others. They share a common Purpose. Alone they are limited. Together they can see everything that can be seen.

We all have a different piece of sky and the truth is, we need each other regardless of how effective and grand we may believe ourselves to be. Others can hold answers for us, and we hold answers for them. What affects me also affects you. YOURS and OURS is really the same word: Y-OURS.

If we can look upon others as 'us' as opposed to 'us' and 'them', we will always collaborate effectively.

Change 'you' in conversation to 'I' whenever we are talking about our own experience.

For example, we might say something like, 'You know when you say "hello" to someone and they ignore you, you feel so rejected.' Changing the pronoun would sound more like, 'When I say "hello" to someone and they ignore me, I feel so rejected.' Immediately we start to take more responsibility for our actions and feelings as opposed to blaming others. This paves the way for greater collaboration and unity.

When dealing with people we find difficult, think 'us'. Treat them as if we are on the same side. You may feel that this is impossible. Every bone in your body might be telling you 'They are not on my side! We are different!' but treat them as if 'they' are 'us' anyway. Even trying to will diminish your stress and the situation will become easier.

Let's assume you disagree with your partner. They may want one thing and you the direct opposite. You may feel rejected, frustrated or angry; however, try treating them as if you were on the same side; as if you wanted the same ultimate outcome; as if you had a common Purpose, and see where it leads. Usually the emphasis of the conversation moves from 'How do I prove myself right?' to 'What's the highest possibility for us both/all?'

But don't believe me. Apply it and see what happens.

Resistance

What to ourselves in Passion we propose,
the passion ending doth the Purpose lose
William Shakespeare

More often than not, whenever we are about to make a big leap forward in our lives, resistance shows its face and tries to put us off. I have not yet come across anybody, myself included, who does not experience this. The final element of the toolkit is perhaps the most important part; because you will, on occasion, feel resistance. What's resistance? Just at the crucial moment of decision; at the crux of a conversation where we are required to go further, become more honest, share our feelings; we are about to make a breakthrough or anything else that makes us feel vulnerable, do we:

- Get hungry
- Get tired
- Get bored
- Get thirsty
- Switch off
- Want to finish
- Find our mind wandering
- Want to leave the room
- Get distracted
- Bury ourselves in work

- Do anything instead of working
- Light a cigarette

That's resistance.

Sometimes we sabotage ourselves in more radical ways. People twist their ankles and stub their toes just when they are about to make a step forward. They miss flights and therefore the meeting, which would help them take off. They lose their telephones as they are about to expand their communication abilities. Forget their wallets when prosperity issues show themselves. All these are completely normal, but not very helpful.

Such classic self-sabotage techniques are the ways we adopt of avoiding completing and moving on. There may be many different reasons why we do this. Essentially, I believe, it is because the next stage is unknown and that can mean uncertainty: 'better the devil you know' some say. In my experience what lies at the other side of completion is 'the angel we have yet to meet'. Although, if all we do is fall prey to our resistance strategies, we will never get that far. Remember, 'It is our light, not our darkness that most frightens us.' As we open ourselves up to greater and greater possibilities in our lives, those little niggling doubts that we keep to ourselves start to surface. Why? Because they have no place in the landscape of the new you. Some things we just have to let go. We cannot become a captain and still do the work of a lieutenant.

When I was a child I was dyslexic; this gave me a lot of problems at school. I overcame the difficulty with help but it left me with a behavioural scar: I hated to be judged on anything I had written. My handwriting was practically illegible and therefore my work was almost unreadable; this translated to my homework and exams, both of which I avoided like the plague and so did poorly at school. I got through school with the bare minimum of results and even managed to get into university; however, my habits stayed with me. You can imagine how hard it was for me when I sat down to write this book. Huge levels of resistance, like a tidal wave, came up in me.

I was very familiar with the material for the book, having conceived of the Purpose / Attitude / Means programme and having delivered it in seminars. I also knew beyond any doubt that it worked and gave tremendous benefit to people. The moment I sat down to write, though, I judged and criticised myself for every word. I found it tiring, frustrating and soul-destroying, and yet very little could speak louder of my Purpose than helping others find theirs. It all came to a head one day when I realised that I had to move through this barrier one way or another.

I sat myself down and gave myself a stiff talking to. I said, 'I am going to write this book. If it means writing one sentence per day until it is finished, binding the book together by hand, going out into the street, giving it to someone, coming home; writing one sentence per day, binding the book together by hand, going out again to hand it to someone else, and on and on, until there is a critical mass of Purpose-driven people in this world, that is what I will do. Nothing will stop me.'

Since that day I have been able to write. I have encountered gusts of resistance, but they never last long and I always find a way through. If fulfilling our Purpose is more important to us than our resistance strategies, we will always find a way through. And if you are reading this, you know that it worked.

A saboteur is only successful if they cannot be seen. Once we become aware of our favourite forms of resistance we develop clarity and a greater sense of compassion towards ourselves. We see the surfacing of such behaviours as familiar, they come and go like the seasons so it doesn't really pay to fight them, only to find a way to work with them effectively. I used to find my own resistance patterns very frustrating. Now they are clear indicators of a way forward. As they surface I know that I am close to making a breakthrough and the nature of the resistance indicates the nature of the breakthrough.

Here some peaceful ways to go beyond them. I have used three classic self-sabotage tactics as examples, some from my own experience, some I share with others, with my chosen strategies for overcoming them.

1. *Distraction*

Symptoms: I fill my time with unimportant details and kid myself that other things need to take priority.

Strategy: Fill in a behaviour map.

Choose the word that for you represents the opposite of distraction, and action that.

Not distracted = focus, motivation, concentration, centredness.

I chose 'focus'; here's how I would action that. *If I were to be focused 8, 9 or 10 out of 10 now I would probably:*

- **Think** *things like What's next? Let's go deeper. I'm loving this.*
- **Say** *things like: 'Keep silent. Listen. Only speak from Purpose.'*
- **Feel** *things like: Clear, open, quiet, peaceful, clean, at ease.*
- **Do** *things like: Continue with the task before me until completion.*

I realise that my habits of distraction do not get me where I want to go, and my task will not get done on its own. If I do not complete what is important, it will come back again and again until I do. Now is better than later. If I can complete it peacefully, so much the better.

The guiding principle I therefore apply here is:

Do what needs to be done.

2. *Doubt*

Symptoms: Thinking things like, I can't do this. It's not going to work. What's the point? It's boring. It's never-ending. I need a break.

Strategy: Refocus on my Purpose statement.

My moods will come and go like the weather. Within that, however, is a constant truth, which is my Purpose. If I choose to trust that over and above how I feel, I can move through my moment of resistance, like holding fast during a storm, maintaining the same direction.

- I become aware that my mood is distracting me from my Purpose.
- I reconnect with my Purpose and my reason for doing what I am doing.
- I choose to re-engage with what is meaningful over what is not.

The following questions are helpful:

- Why am I doing this task?
- What and whom does it serve?
- Does it serve my Purpose? How?
- Is it the task that is unfulfilling or is it me?
- Is the task worthy?
- What would my Purpose do now?
- If my Purpose were to fulfil this task it would do something like . . .

> *Guiding principle: Trust truth over mood.*

3. *Resentment*

Symptoms: I think things like, Other people don't have to go through this, why should I? I have distracting physical desires such as getting hungry, tired, becoming listless, jumpy or sexually distracted.

Strategy: Track the feeling to source.

- Acknowledge the feeling.
- Trace it back.
- Identify with it.

As Marie Curie said, 'Nothing is to be feared, it is to be understood.' Applying that principle to my resistance, I sit in the feeling, not trying to change it or alter it in any way. I give it my full awareness, watching how and where it affects me: the sensations in my body, the quality of my thoughts. I then trace it back to its source. I follow it behind all the symptoms, further and further back until I can touch its source. I know that I am at the source when I can strongly identify with the feeling. I can call it by name with 10 out of 10 clarity, and I know where it has affected me throughout my life. When I hit this point it dissipates, like a glass that shatters when a high note is sung into it.

If I give it my full attention, the process takes about ten minutes. It is a good investment of time.

> ***Guiding principle: Face into it.***

A Final Thought

A sailing boat or an aeroplane in flight is constantly buffeted by winds and currents. It is off course 99 per cent of the time. What brings it to its destination is that throughout all the moments where it is off course the pilot seeks its true direction. Our moods, our internal 'weather', can often take us off track if we let them. In those times we can doubt the veracity of our Purpose and tell ourselves stories that discredit the truth we discovered. In that moment we have to ask ourselves, 'What do I trust, my mood or my Purpose?'

Reconnecting with our Purpose helps us distinguish between what is true and what is our resistance. All forms of distraction ultimately stem from doubt and fear. It is very easy to doubt the veracity of our decisions when we feel tired, uninspired, have just suffered a setback or are under the weather for some reason. If we stray from what is important every time our mood changes we are treating ourselves as a victim of circumstance instead of its creator. So, do we choose to be a passenger or a pilot?

Choosing to be a pilot means the moment you feel out of touch with your Purpose, seek it again. Reconnect with it any way you can; come back on course. I find it useful to ask myself questions to check in. Some like to listen to the piece of music that reminds them of it. Some perform an action. What's *your* way?

1. *List your three classic forms of sabotage/resistance.*

2. *Choose a strategy for each. Base these ideas on some of the work we've just done; perhaps some strategies will come to you from other activities we've completed in this book.*

3. *How will you make sure you stick to this strategy when resistance shows itself and you don't feel like it?*

If ever you are in doubt, simply ask yourself,
'Does this serve my Purpose?'
If it does, do it.
If it doesn't, don't.

Moving Beyond the
Known

Your life is not predetermined, it is created by you every single moment. When we wake up in the morning we are not given a script to follow that day. Within certain parameters, we make it up as we go along, we improvise. Naming our Purpose and living it through our Attitude and Means simply invites you to improvise within a different set of parameters. Ones that encourage you to give the best of yourself and to live the highest possibility you can muster in every moment – your 8, 9, 10 life.

You are the writer, director and actor of your life.
It's your story.
Living your Purpose helps you make sure it's one
you want to be in.

Once we start to action our goals and ask Purpose to speak through us we come to the end of our experience, as we know it, and start a new beginning. We have never lived our Purpose consciously before, so our lives will definitely change. We start to look at the world in a clearer and more complete way. We ask ourselves different questions and

>>>

we have a greater respect and understanding for others. We evolve into our highest selves.

Most people live tight inside their comfort zones, rarely dipping their toe into the water that takes them beyond. As we start to explore our Purpose more and more, we will go well beyond our previous experience of the world and know ourselves in a new way. The reality is that when we move outside the comfort zone and become perfectly at ease there, we become more solid, grounded, effective and fulfilled. We learn to walk on shifting sands. However, to get there sometimes requires us dealing with the part of us that is afraid of change.

The process we have undergone is both honest and profound. When we look at our deepest truth in the eye and then start to embrace it we automatically make adjustments in our lives. Our truth has a compelling quality about it, a sense of 'rightness', and we feel like we have come home to ourselves. That truth, that Purpose, is our love expressed. As that is released more and more we develop a deeper love and respect for ourselves and, as a consequence, for others. Life becomes richer and more meaningful and the boundaries of work and play begin to blur. Every part of life moves towards being a simple expression and playground for that deeper love.

When I see people who are living their Purpose they have a quality of inner acceptance and peace. They seem to hold a quiet greatness without showing it, and they are free.

A free person is one who can make a path as much as

follow one. A person who knows their own mind without having to be rebellious; one who understands that there is a bigger picture in the world that they fit into. The world does not revolve around them, they are simply taking part in ways that are natural to them. A free person fundamentally understands that all people are equal, and that no hierarchy, social standing, wealth or intellectual capability changes that. They see people and situations for what they are, without having to judge them as 'good' and 'bad'.

A free person understands that this is their world and fearlessly takes responsibility for it. They are a force of nature.

For example, one man named Jeremy Gilley discovered that there has never been a single day of global ceasefire in the history of humanity. Not one day when someone has not left their house in the morning with the express purpose of killing someone else. He felt that it was about time that we had at least one day. He started working out of his old room in his mother's house with a telephone and a computer. With no financial backing or resources, and having left school at sixteen with a minimal education, Jeremy set out to build the case for the day's creation, and document his journey on film. He spoke to everybody. The United Nations, world leaders, heads of industry and business, spiritual leaders and prominent entertainers. Two years later and four days before the 11 September attacks, UN member states unanimously adopted a day of global ceasefire and non-violence on the

United Nations International Day of Peace, 21 September annually. One day where arms can be lain down and aid and healing given to those in need. A pause in conflict to reflect on and celebrate the possibility of peace.*

One free person can change the world.

As we start to live our Purpose in the world we create an updraught for those around us, creating an extra 71 per cent lift. We literally become generators of community. Purpose is the cornerstone to the next level of our evolution as a species and functional community is how that manifests. Your taking this step opens the next chapter of your life. You are saying 'Yes' to a higher possibility for yourself and others, for humanity as a whole.

If we can live in alignment with others, like geese, focused on a common Purpose there will be peace.

How much does that say 'Yes' to you out of 10?

* www.peaceoneday.org.

Index

May Purpose Guide You

Please share your Purpose and stories online at
www.one-purpose.com